The Evolution of Spanish Past Forms

The Evolution of Spanish Past Forms examines how Spanish past forms have changed diachronically.

With examples from Medieval Spanish, Golden Age Spanish, and Modern Spanish literary works, this book demonstrates how language is dynamic and susceptible to change. The past forms considered here include the preterit, the imperfect, the imperfect progressive with *estar* (temporal to be), the present perfect, the imperfect progressive with other auxiliary verbs, the preterit progressive with *estar*, and the preterit progressive with other auxiliary verbs.

This book will be of interest to scholars and graduate students investigating tense and aspect phenomena in Spanish and other languages, grammaticalization processes, and language variation and change.

Gibran Delgado-Díaz teaches Spanish Linguistics at the University of Puerto Rico, Mayagüez.

Routledge Studies in Hispanic and Lusophone Linguistics
Series Editor: Dale Koike, University of Texas at Austin

The Routledge Studies in Hispanic and Lusophone Linguistics series provides a showcase for the latest research on Spanish and Portuguese Linguistics. It publishes select research monographs on various topics in the field, reflecting strands of current interest.

Titles in the series:

Spanish in the United States
Attitudes and Variation
Edited by Scott M. Alvord and Gregory L. Thompson

Spanish in Health Care
Policy, Practice and Pedagogy in Latino Health
Glenn A. Martínez

Los castellanos del Perú
historia, variación y contacto lingüístico
Luis Andrade Ciudad y Sandro Sessarego (eds.)

Language Patterns in Spanish and Beyond
Structure, Context and Development
Edited by Juan J. Colomina-Almiñana and Sandro Sessarego

The Evolution of Spanish Past Forms
Gibran Delgado-Díaz

For more information about this series please visit:
www.routledge.com/Routledge-Studies-in-Hispanic-and-Lusophone-Linguistics/book-series/RSHLL

The Evolution of Spanish Past Forms

Gibran Delgado-Díaz

Series Editor: Dale A. Koike
Spanish List Advisor: Javier Muñoz-Basols

LONDON AND NEW YORK

First published 2021
by Routledge
2 Park Square, Milton Park, Abingdon, Oxon OX14 4RN

and by Routledge
52 Vanderbilt Avenue, New York, NY 10017

Routledge is an imprint of the Taylor & Francis Group, an informa business

© 2021 Gibran Delgado-Díaz

The right of Gibran Delgado-Díaz to be identified as author of this work has been asserted by him in accordance with sections 77 and 78 of the Copyright, Designs and Patents Act 1988.

All rights reserved. No part of this book may be reprinted or reproduced or utilised in any form or by any electronic, mechanical, or other means, now known or hereafter invented, including photocopying and recording, or in any information storage or retrieval system, without permission in writing from the publishers.

Trademark notice: Product or corporate names may be trademarks or registered trademarks, and are used only for identification and explanation without intent to infringe.

British Library Cataloguing-in-Publication Data
A catalogue record for this book is available from the British Library

Library of Congress Cataloging-in-Publication Data
A catalog record has been requested for this book

ISBN: 978-0-367-32247-2 (hbk)
ISBN: 978-0-429-31749-1 (ebk)

Typeset in Times New Roman
by Newgen Publishing UK

Contents

List of tables vii
List of figures ix

1 Introduction 1
   1.1 Introduction 1
   1.2 Aspect in Spanish 3
      1.2.1 Factors that influence aspect 5
   1.3 Summary of the Spanish tense and aspectual systems 10

2 Grammaticalization Theory 11
   2.1 Introduction 11
   2.2 Grammaticalization 11
   2.3 Grammaticalization Theory 15
   2.4 Grammaticalization in the diachronic axis 16
   2.5 Grammaticalization and the Spanish past forms 18
   2.6 Conclusions 23

3 Previous studies on Spanish past forms 24
   3.1 Introduction 24
   3.2 The preterit 24
      3.2.1 Aspectual function 24
      3.2.2 Lexical aspect 29
      3.2.3 Discourse functions 31
      3.2.4 Summary of the preterit 32
   3.3 The imperfect 33
      3.3.1 Aspectual function 33
      3.3.2 Lexical semantics 35
      3.3.3 Discourse functions 37
      3.3.4 Review of the imperfect 38

3.4 Present perfect 39
    3.4.1 Aspectual functions 39
    3.4.2 Lexical semantics 43
    3.4.3 Discourse function 44
    3.4.4 Summary of the present perfect 46
3.5 *Imperfect progressive* 47
    3.5.1 Aspectual function 47
    3.5.2 Lexical semantic 48
    3.5.3 Discourse function 49
    3.5.4 Summary of the imperfect progressive 50
3.6 *Preterit progressive* 51
    3.6.1 Aspectual function 51
    3.6.2 Lexical semantic 52
    3.6.3 Discourse function 53
    3.6.4 Summary of the preterit progressive 54
3.7 *Summary of the previous investigations* 54

4 The study   58
4.1 *Rationale for the present study* 58
    4.1.1 Research questions 59
4.2 *Methodology* 59
    4.2.1 The diachronic data 59
    4.2.2 Coding scheme 60
    4.2.3 Analysis 77

5 Results   79
5.1 *Introduction* 79
5.2 *The imperfect* 79
5.3 *The preterit* 89
5.4 *Present perfect* 99
5.5 *Progressive constructions* 102

6 Discussion and conclusions   112
6.1 *Introduction* 112
6.2 *Patterns of variation* 112
6.3 *Grammaticalization Theory and language change* 119
6.4 *Conclusions* 126

Bibliography   129
Index   139

Tables

1.1	Vendler's (1957) verb classes	5
2.1	Grammaticalization chain or cline of the compound past	18
2.2	Multivariate analysis of the factors that predict the use of the present progressive with *estar* in Old Spanish, 17th century and 19th century	19
3.1	Results of the statistical analysis according to the time period	41
4.1	Novels analyzed in the diachronic study	60
4.2	Example of normalization formula with ser 'to be'	73
4.3	Example coding of the multiple response set	78
5.1	Distribution of the imperfect across centuries	80
5.2	Mixed-effects logistic regressions models for the imperfect according to period	81
5.3	Constraint hierarchy of the imperfect according to period	86
5.4	Aspectual function of the imperfect according to period	86
5.5	Distribution of the imperfect according to type of information and period	87
5.6	Distribution of the imperfect according to priming and period	88
5.7	Distribution of the imperfect in Golden Age Spanish according to the lexical semantic of the verb	89
5.8	Distribution of the preterit across centuries	89
5.9	Mixed-effects logistic regressions models for the preterit according to period	90
5.10	Constraint hierarchy of the preterit according to period	95
5.11	Distribution of the preterit across centuries according to type of information and aspectual function	95
5.12	Distribution of the preterit according to aspectual function, priming and type of information in Medieval Spanish	97

5.13	Distribution of the preterit in Golden Age Spanish according to specificity of the subject, grammatical person, and aspectual function	98
5.14	Distribution of the present perfect across centuries	99
5.15	Distribution of the present perfect across centuries according to lexical semantics	100
5.16	Distribution of the present perfect across centuries according to grammatical person	101
5.17	Distribution of the progressive constructions across centuries	102
5.18	Distribution of the imperfect progressive with *estar* across centuries	103
5.19	Distribution of the preterit progressive with *estar* across centuries	103
5.20	Progressive constructions distribution of the progressive constructions regarding locative co-occurrence, adjacency, association, and fusion	104
5.21	Distribution of the imperfect progressive with other auxiliary verbs across centuries	106
5.22	Distribution of the preterit progressive with other auxiliary verbs across centuries	109
6.1	Constraint hierarchy of the imperfect according to period	120
6.2	Constraint hierarchy of the preterit according to period	120
6.3	Comparison between the present progressive with the past progressives	123

Figures

1.1	Aspectual classifications	3
2.1	Grammaticalization process of the future construction *be going to*	14
2.2	Grammaticalization path of the future	16
3.1	Representation of the aspectual functions according to the past form	55
5.1	Conditional tree of the factors that influence the imperfect in Medieval Spanish	82
5.2	Conditional tree of the factors that influence the imperfect in Golden Age Spanish	83
5.3	Conditional tree of the factors that influence the imperfect in Modern Spanish	85
5.4	Conditional tree of the factors that influence the preterit in Medieval Spanish	92
5.5	Conditional tree of the factors that influence the preterit in Golden Age Spanish	93
5.6	Conditional tree of the factors that influence the preterit in Modern Spanish	94
6.1	Distribution of the preterit in progressive and habitual functions and the imperfect with a perfective function	114
6.2	Representation of the aspectual functions of each form according to previous investigations	116
6.3	Representation of the aspectual function according to each construction	117
6.4	Representation of the perfective aspectual function exemplar	121
6.5	Grammaticalization order of the Spanish progressive forms	124
6.6	Grammaticalization path of the progressive constructions	125
6.7	Overall distribution of *andar* 'to walk', *ir* 'to go', and *estar*	126

1 Introduction

1.1 Introduction

This book examines Spanish past-time expressions diachronically (i.e., in the historic dimension) within literary works with the purpose of tracking past-time expression constraints through time. This investigation considers the past-expressions illustrated in (1.1). Additionally, the data derived from literary works from Medieval Spanish, Golden Age Spanish, and Modern Spanish, following Torres Cacoullos' (2012, 2015) methodology. Spanish past forms were chosen because, although they generally express different aspectual meanings (i.e., aspect is defined as "...different ways of viewing the internal temporal constituency of a situation" [Comrie, 1976: 3]), there are instances when they convey overlapping aspectual notions. For example, previous investigations have found that the imperfect progressive with *estar* (1.1c) and the imperfect (1.1a) can be used to convey a past habitual function (i.e., an event that was repeated in the past) or past progressive (i.e., an ongoing event in the past) (Bybee, Perkins, & Pagliuca, 1994; Delgado-Díaz, in press; Lamanna, 2008, 2012). Moreover, the preterit (1.1b) and present perfect (1.1e) can be used to express single completed events in the past (i.e., perfective aspect) (Hernández, 2004; Howe & Schwenter, 2008; Schwenter 1994; Schwenter & Torres Cacoullos, 2008; among many others).

(1.1) a. ...cuando esto ovo fecho, odredes lo que *fablava*. (Cantar del Mio Cid)
...when he had done this, they heard what he said.
b. *Fabló* mio Cid, el que en buen ora cinxo espada. (Cantar Del Mio Cid)
Mio Cid spoke, the one that in good time took his sword in arms.

c. ...se fueron hacia la parte donde aún **estaba hablando**...
    (El Quijote)
    ...they went to the place where they were still talking...
d. Esta tarde **estuvo hablando** con él... (Doña Perfecta)
    I was talking to him this afternoon...
e. Ella me mira a veces con la ardiente mirada de que ya
    he hablado a usted. (Pepita Jiménez)
    Sometimes she looks at me with the burning look I have
    already told you.

Despite the various meanings that can be expressed through Spanish past-time expressions, previous investigations tend to focus only on a handful of forms in a dichotomous fashion. For example, most investigations examine the following oppositions: preterit vs imperfect, preterit vs present perfect, and imperfect vs imperfect progressive. This methodology assumes a form-function symmetry, it does not consider the complexity of the past aspectual system and the fact that past forms can share common aspectual meanings (Delgado-Díaz, in press; Poplack, 2018). In fact, Poplack (2018) rejects a form-function symmetry arguing that syntactic variation may entail neutralized functional distinctions. Consequently, researchers must include all the possible forms that may share aspectual meanings to present a complete picture of the envelope of variation (Delgado-Díaz, in press; Poplack & Tagliamonte, 1999). Therefore, the present investigation includes all forms that express past events. More specifically, we aim to determine if the linguistic and extra-linguistic factors that constrain the use of these past expressions change through time. Additionally, we intent to study which forms interact within the progressive, habitual, and perfective aspectual domains (Bybee et al., 1994; Comrie, 1976)

It is worth highlighting that this investigation is guided by Grammaticalization Theory, which makes predictions on how lexical items gain and continue to develop further grammatical meaning. Similarly, it proposes a hypothesis about language change in the diachronic axis (Bybee et al., 1994; Heine, 2003; Hopper & Traugott, 2003).

The next section of this chapter is dedicated to aspect in Spanish because one goal is to determine which forms interact with each other on past aspectual domains. The study focuses on habitual, progressive, and perfective aspectual function, as defined by Comrie (1976) and Bybee et al. (1994). In addition, the following sections also discuss the different factors that influence the choice of past-expression in Spanish because some may overlap with aspect.

1.2 Aspect in Spanish

Comrie (1976) defined aspect as "...different ways of viewing the internal temporal constituency of a situation" (p.3). According to this scholar, the notion of aspect expresses the speaker's point of view regarding a particular event or situation. By this definition, aspect is an internal characteristic of the event and does not necessarily make any reference to the moment of speech. Grammatical aspect refers to the aspectual information provided by morphology (see Figure 1.1). Comrie (1976) proposed the aspectual classifications presented in Figure 1.1, which demonstrates that aspect can be categorically divided as perfective or imperfective. The perfective category entails past events that have an end point and are completed while imperfect entails situations that are ongoing and/or incomplete (Comrie, 1976: 19). According to Comrie (1976), perfective events are categorized as being seen from an outside viewpoint while imperfective events are categorized as being viewed from the inside. Comrie's (1976) categorization includes other readings of the imperfect, such as habitual, continuative, progressive, and non-progressive.

Regarding the imperfective classifications, a habitual function is defined as an event that is repeated during an extensive period of time, in such a manner that it becomes an inherent characteristic of that event (Comrie, 1976). The example in (1.2a) illustrates a habitual aspectual function in which the event of *pasaban* 'would spend' occurred occasionally. The progressive aspectual function is considered to present an event as ongoing in the reference time (Bybee et al., 1994). The fragment in (1.2b) shows a use of the imperfect *hacía* 'he was doing' in a progressive context which is modified by *mientras* 'while'. On the contrary, non-progressiveness refers to a nearly permanent state of affairs (Comrie,

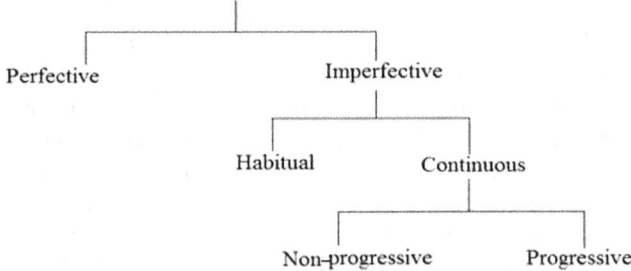

Figure 1.1 Aspectual classifications (Comrie, 1976: 25)

4 Introduction

1976). Comrie (1976) gives the example *the sphinx stands by the Nile River* as a non-progressive reading. He added that progressiveness and non-progressiveness differ in a temporary/permanent distinction. On the other hand, continuous is defined as a type of more general progressive in the sense that it can be used with progressive situations but can include stative predicates. However, Bybee et al. (1994) reject the categories continuous and non-progressive, because they did not find grammatical items that express these meanings in their data. Consequently, the present study focuses on the aspectual categories habitual, progressive, and perfective.

(1.2) a. ...y los demás días se los *pasaban* en flores. (El Quijote)
...and the other days they would spend on flowers.
b. ...mientras él *hacía* frente en Madrid al formidable empuje de los acreedores. (Doña Perfecta)
...while he was facing the formidable push of the creditors in Madrid.

This book focuses on Spanish past-expression for the following reasons: first, little is known about the evolution of these past-expressions in Spanish. Penny (2000) stated that the preterit and imperfect were inherited from Latin; but little is known about the emergence and evolution of the past progressive constructions. In addition, Penny (2000) does not mention if the factors that predict the use of the preterit and imperfect changed through time. Second, most studies on Spanish past-expressions focus on dichotomous pairs; for example, the preterit and imperfect (Baker & Quesada, 2011; Delgado-Díaz, 2014, 2018b; Quesada, 2013;), the preterit and present perfect (Henderson, 2010; Howe, 2006; Menegotto, 2008; Ocampo, 2008; Rodríguez-Louro, 2009; Schwenter & Torres Cacoullos, 2008; among many others), and the imperfect and imperfect progressive (Chaston, 1991; Lamanna, 2008, 2012; Koontz-Garboden, 1999; López-Otero & Cuza, 2020; Mrak, 1998; Quesada, 1993; Ramos-Pellicia, 1999). These types of designs assume that these structures operate in pairs without interacting with other forms; for example, changes in the imperfect progressive will not affect the preterit progressive. In addition, this methodology assumes that there is form-function symmetry. However, Poplack (2018) argues that variation entails neutralized contexts and form-function asymmetry. Finally, there are few investigations that focus on the preterit progressive with *estar* (Delgado-Díaz, in press; Westfall, 1995, 2003). It is worth highlighting that Westfall's (1995, 2003) investigations are descriptive which may not represent actual uses of this construction.

The lack of quantitative studies in the preterit progressive with *estar* makes it impossible to determine if this structure is variable and what factors constrain that variation.

The present investigation argues that the best way to study these structures is by focusing on function rather than on form; that is, to investigate the aspectual function (i.e., habitual, progressive, and perfective) these constructions convey. This allows us to determine which aspectual domains are more prone to variation. Additionally, focusing on function can present a better picture regarding the usage pattern of past aspectual forms. It is worth mentioning that this type of analysis may include other forms as well, such as the simple present, the pluscuamperfecto, among other forms, that may express progressive, habitual, and/or perfective aspectual functions. Finally, this type of analysis does not assume form-function symmetry; on the contrary, it anticipates form-function asymmetry and neutralized contexts.

1.2.1 Factors that influence aspect

Aspect is compositional in the sense that a single verb does not provide the whole aspectual meaning (Ocampo, 2008: 80). This observation means that there are several other factors that contribute and influence the choice between these different aspectual forms. This section reviews some of those factors.

One factor that is said to influence the use of past forms is lexical semantics (this factor is also known as Aktionsart or lexical aspect). This factor is based on Vendler's (1957) verb classes which include four different verb types: states, activities, accomplishments, and achievements (see Table 1.1). States and activities are atelic, which implies that the event does not have an inherent end point. These two verbs are distinguished by dynamicity: in which states are not dynamic while activities are. On the other hand, accomplishments and achievements are telics, which means that the event has an inherent end point. Duration distinguishes between accomplishments and achievements: the first are

Table 1.1 Vendler's (1957) verb classes

Predicate Example	State To know	Activity To run	Accomplishment To reach	Achievement To find
Dynamicity	-	+	+	+
Telicity	-	-	+	+
Punctuality	-	-	-	+

durative while the latter are punctual. The example in (1.3a) illustrates a stative verb *eran* 'they were', (1.3b) shows an activity verb *caminaba* 'she was walking', (1.3c) demonstrates an accomplishment verb *recibió* 'he received', and (1.3d) illustrates an achievement verb *llegó* 'he arrived'.

(1.3)   a.   ...porque en efecto **eran** hombres como nosotros...
           (El Quijote)
           ...because they were indeed men the same as us...

      b.   ...y **caminaba** con un vestido corto... (Pepita Jimena)
           ...and she was walking with a short dress...

      c.   **Recibió** cartas mi tío. (Los Locos de Valencia)
           My uncle received letters.

      d.   ...cuando **llegó** a San Pero el buen Campeador. (El Cantar del Mio Cid)
           ...when the good Champion arrived at Saint Peter.

These different types of verbs tend to influence the selection of the past form. For instance, the Lexical Aspect Hypothesis (Andersen & Shirai, 1996) predicts that the imperfect emerges with state and activity verbs, and the preterit appears with accomplishment and achievement verbs in second language learners of Spanish. Similar predictions have been proposed for Spanish native speakers, stating that the imperfect is compatible with state and activity verbs because these are durative and atelic. The preterit tends to be used more frequently with accomplishment and achievement verbs because these are telic (Acero, 1990; Alcina Franch & Blecua, 1975; RAE, 1973, 2010). The present perfect is compatible with states and activity verbs because these verbs are durative and do not have an inherent end point (Burgo, 2010; Dumont, 2013; Hernández, 2004). The imperfect progressive with *estar* and the preterit progressive with *estar* tend to be used more frequently with activity and accomplishment verbs since they are dynamic and durative (Quesada, 1993; Westfall, 1995, 2000).

It should be noted that lexical aspect can be modified by the verb's argument structure (i.e., the verbal phrase) (Dowty, 1977, 1979, 1986; Salas-Gonzáles, 1996; Verkuyl, 1972, 2005, 2012). For example, an activity verb like *comer* 'to eat' can become an accomplishment as in *comer una manzana* 'to eat one apple'. Similarly, the following prepositional phrase was considered since an activity as *caminar* 'to walk' can become an accomplishment if it is modified by *para* 'to, for, on, etc.'. For example, *caminar para la casa* 'walking to the house' would be considered an accomplishment since the prepositional phrase *para*

Introduction 7

la casa establishes an end point to *caminar*. Consequently, the present study considered the whole context (i.e., verbs and their arguments) while coding for this variable.

Several researchers have made different criticisms to Vendler's (1957) verb classes (De Miguel, 1999; Dowty, 1972; Verkuyl, 1972). Filip (2011) mentioned that some of these criticisms pertain to stative verbs. According to some scholars (De Miguel, 1999; Filip, 2011), some epistemic verbs (*know* and *understand*) can change their aspectual class from stative to achievement when they co-occur with adverbs such as *once* and *suddenly* (Filip, 2011). Consequently, some scholars include cognitive and perception verbs (Aaron, 2006; De Miguel, 1999). For instance, Aaron (2006: 40) made the distinction between stative (*sentirse* 'to feel', *estar* and *ser* 'to be', etc.), cognitive (*pensar* 'to think', *creer* 'to believe', etc.), and perception (*oír* 'to hear', *ver* 'to see', etc.) verbs. This distinction is important because cognitive and perception verbs are different in contrast to states. For instance, cognitive verbs describe the speaker's own psychological disposition to a speech event (Fetzer & Johansson, 2010: 243) and perception verbs describe what can be perceived by the five senses (i.e., see, hear, smell, feel, and taste) (Ibarretxe-Antuñano, 1999). Furthermore, previous investigations on perception verbs differentiate between passive perception (John *heard* some music) and active perception (John *listened* to some music) stating that active perception requires a certain amount of activity by the subject (Helle, 2006; Ibarretxe-Antuñano, 1999). This means that both cognitive and perception verbs can have a dynamic interpretation (Filip, 2011; Helle, 2006; Ibarretxe-Antuñano, 1999). This implies that dynamicity can be viewed as a spectrum where state verbs have no dynamicity, cognitive verbs show cognitive activity, perception verbs can require some activity; whereas activity, accomplishment, and achievement verbs are dynamic. Consequently, this investigation made the distinction between cognitive and perception verbs in order to account for these nuances.

Another factor that influences the past form choice is type of information, known as the Discourse Hypothesis (Hopper, 1979). This hypothesis predicts that the preterit is used more frequently with foreground information and the imperfect with background information (Hopper, 1979). According to Hopper (1979), foreground information recounts the events of the narrative; it can be interpreted as the chronological order of the story. In contrast, background information provides descriptions in the narrative (Silva-Corvalán, 1983) or events that are not temporally anchored (Slabakova, 2002). For instance, *robó* 'he stole' in example (1.4a) would be considered foreground information because it moves the event forward while *era* 'it was' (1.4b) would be background information because it provides a description of Mahoma's idol. Additionally, previous investigations have found that the imperfect progressive can also express background information (Gonzales, 1995; Mrak, 1998; Silva-Corvalán, 1983).

(1.4)   ...y cuando en Allende *robó* (a) aquel ídolo de Mahoma, que *era* (b) todo de oro... (El Quijote)
...and when in Allende he stole Mahoma's idol, which was made of gold.

Lexical semantics and the type of information are not mutually exclusive. Bardovi-Harlig (2000) proposes that both hypotheses can interact because foregrounded events are characterized by being punctual and completed; they are semantic properties that relate to accomplishments and achievements (Bardovi-Harlig, 2000: 300). This argument can be extended to background events which are characterized by being durative and incomplete, notions that reflect state and activity verbs. Furthermore, Bardovi-Harlig (2000) stated that sometimes it is difficult to distinguish between both hypotheses.

Another factor that may influence the choice of past forms is the specificity of the event (Montrul & Slabakova, 2003; Rodríguez-Ramalle, 2005). For instance, Montrul and Slabakova (2003) argued that the preterit can have a specific or existential reading while the imperfect can have a generic or universal reading. According to this view, example (1.5a) means that a single specific dinosaur ate kelp. On the contrary, example (1.5b) would mean that dinosaurs, as a whole species, ate kelp (Montrul & Slabakova, 2003). According to Montrul and Slabakova (2003), specific events are compatible with the preterit because this form does not allow the repetition of the event. Generic events, on the other hand, are compatible with the imperfect because they allow the repetition of the event. This variable has not been applied to the other forms; consequently, it is unknown how this factor affects other past aspectual forms.

(1.5)   a. El dinosaurio *comió* algas. (Montrul & Slabakova, 2003: 359)
The dinosaur ate kelp. (Translation taken from Montrul & Slabakova, 2003: 359)

b. El dinosaurio *comía* algas. (Montrul & Slabakova, 2003: 359)
Dinosaurs used to eat kelp. (Translation taken from Montrul & Slabakova, 2003: 359)

However, this variable is problematic because it includes circular arguments and subjective notions. As for the circular arguments,

Montrul and Slabakova (2003) argued that each form carries a particular meaning: the preterit is specific while the imperfect is generic. This argumentation implies that the verb argument and the type of discourse do not provide any information and that the preterit and imperfect do not show any variation regarding this factor. In addition, this claim assumes a form-function symmetry in which each form expresses a particular interpretation. As for the subjective notions, generic events are defined as actions that allow its repetition while specific events do not. These definitions may not allow to systematic and objectively code in spoken data.

Consequently, this factor was modified in the present dissertation to avoid circular arguments and to have an objective coding criterion. Therefore, this study focuses on the specificity of the subject since the subject provides an objective coding criterion. This decision is based on Montrul and Slabakova's (2003) as well as Rodríguez-Ramalle's (2005) definitions of specific and generic subjects. These scholars defined specific events as those that have definite subjects. Definite subjects are those in which the agent can be identified with a specific person, animal, or object, for example, *yo* 'I', *tú* 'you', *el niño* 'the boy', etc. A specific subject is illustrated in (1.6a) in which Pepe is the subject of *salió* 'he got out'. On the contrary, "generic" subjects can be defined, following Rodríguez-Ramalle's (2005) and Montrul and Slabakova's (2003) definitions, as indefinite subjects (i.e., *una persona* 'a person', *una muchacha* 'a girl', etc.), or entities that make up a bigger class, such as humans, people, plants, animals, etc. This includes passive/impersonal *se* (*se venden libros* 'books are sold'), or impersonal third person plural constructions (*robaron el banco* 'the bank was robbed') because they do not express a definable subject. The fragment in (1.6b) illustrates a generic subject *todos* 'everyone'. It is worth mentioning that discourse cues were considered when coding for this factor since the indefinite subject can have a definite interpretation. For instance, it was verified if it was the first mention of the subject. It is expected that the preterit is used more frequently with specific subjects because it is more likely to express single completed events (Montrul & Slabakova, 2003). On the contrary, generic subjects will favor the imperfect because they tend to express habitual events (Montrul & Slabakova, 2003). It is not clear how this variable will affect the progressive forms since there is no prior research on this issue.

(1.6) a. Pepe ***salió*** de Puerto Real… (Doña Perfecta)
Pepe got out from Puerto Real…

    b. Todos los que ***estavan*** en aquel palaçio… (Caballero de Zifar)
Everyone that was in the palace…

10 *Introduction*

This section showed that there are different factors that may influence the choice between the different past forms. These include the lexical aspect, the type of information, and the specificity of the subject. This observation may imply that there may be a certain degree of variation because the use of past form is conditioned by different factors.

1.3 Summary of the Spanish tense and aspectual systems

This chapter introduced the object of study which is the Spanish past-time expressions. This includes the preterit, imperfect, present perfect, imperfect progressive with *estar*, preterit progressive with *estar*, and other forms that can express perfective, habitual, and/or progressive aspectual functions. Recall that continuous and non-progressive were not considered in this dissertation, since Bybee et al. (1994) did not find grammatical constructions that express these aspectual notions based on a survey of 79 languages. Other forms, such as the pluscuamperfecto and past progressive with other auxiliary verbs, may be included since the analysis focuses on function. The main goal of the present investigation is to track historical changes regarding Spanish past aspectual forms. Consequently, this book includes a diachronic analysis which allows us to study how these forms change through time. The diachronic data comes from literary works within Medieval Spanish, Golden Age Spanish, and Modern Spanish, following Torres Cacoullos' (2012, 2015) methodology; see chapter 4 for a complete description of the methodology.

Additionally, this chapter showed that the choice between the different past forms may be influenced by different factors, which included lexical semantics, type of information, and specificity of the subject. It was also stated that some forms, such as the past progressives, have not been investigated using some of these factors. In addition, this chapter mentioned that most tense and aspect investigations have studied these forms in dichotomous pairs, which does not account for variation and change outside the pair investigated (Delgado-Díaz, 2018a, in press). Additionally, most previous investigations assume form-function symmetry (Poplack, 2018). Finally, there are few investigations that study the evolution of Spanish past-time expressions. Therefore, the Spanish tense and aspect system requires further investigations with the goal of understanding how past forms interact with each other and evolve. In fact, there may be variable contexts that previous investigations have yet uncovered.

2 Grammaticalization Theory

2.1 Introduction

This chapter discusses grammaticalization mechanisms and Grammaticalization Theory predictions. This theory provides working hypotheses for language change phenomena. Therefore, this chapter aims to explain grammaticalization processes, define Grammaticalization Theory, its hypotheses, and how it can be applied to the study of Spanish past-time expressions. This chapter is organized as follows: the first section discusses grammaticalization mechanisms. The next section defines Grammaticalization Theory, its hypotheses, and how variationist methods can be applied to test these hypotheses. The following section focuses on how grammaticalization can be observed in diachronic data. The last section explains how Grammaticalization Theory can be applied to investigate Spanish past aspectual forms.

2.2 Grammaticalization

Language is a dynamic phenomenon and, as such, it changes over time (Bybee, 2003a, 2010). Some lexical items may shift their categorical status to grammatical morphemes while some grammatical structures are lost, others are created (Bybee, 2003a). Many of these changes can be attributed to grammaticalization. Grammaticalization, as a process, is defined as "the change whereby lexical items serve grammatical functions, and once grammaticalized, continue to develop new grammatical functions" (Hopper & Traugott, 2003: XV). Bybee et al. (1994) added that grammatical morphemes develop out of lexical morphemes or a combination of lexical and/or grammatical morphemes (p.4). These scholars stated that the grammaticalizing material is dependent on the surrounding context and, in many cases, the grammaticalizing material becomes fused with other morphemes. A common example is the synthetic future in Spanish (Aaron, 2006; Bybee, 2015). According to Bybee (2015), this form emerged from the combination of verb + *habēre* 'to have/to hold' with an obligation function in Latin. The example in (2.1) illustrates this future construction. *Habēre* continued to be phonetically reduced and attached to the infinitive. This process resulted in different synthetic future forms: *canter-ò* in Italian, *cantar-é* in Spanish, *cantar-ei* in Portuguese, etc. 'I will sing' (Bybee, 2015: 121).

(2.1) Essere habetis (Bybee, 2015: 121)
       'You will be'

Grammaticalization is unidirectional and consists of certain related mechanisms (Bybee 2003a; Heine 2003). These mechanisms are the following (Bybee, 2003a, Heine, 2003):

i. Semantic bleaching (desemanticalization, semantic reduction)
ii. Generalization (extension, use in new contexts)
iii. Decategorization (loss of morphosyntactic properties)
iv. Erosion (phonetic reduction)

Semantic bleaching refers to the loss of specific lexical meaning (Heine, 2003). For example, the Spanish progressive form *estar* + -ndo originated from a locative source (Torres Cacoullos, 2000, 2012, 2015). In Old Spanish *estar* + -ndo meant to be located performing an action (Bybee et al., 1994, Torres Cacoullos, 2012, 2015). The example in (2.2), taken from Torres Cacoullos (2012) illustrates a specific use of the present progressive in the 13th century, in which the subjects are located at the mills performing an action. The locative meaning is being bleached from the progressive construction since it can be used without co-occurring with locative expressions (Bybee & Torres Cacoullos, 2009; Torres Cacoullos, 2012, 2015). Generalization means that the grammaticalized form can be used in more contexts (Heine, 2003). Bybee (2003a) mentioned that *be going to* in English could only be used to express a movement to a goal by an agent (an agentive subject) in Shakespeare's English. However, this construction began to be extended to *intention* and *prediction* contexts, notions that encompass future meaning. In fact, in present day English *be going to* can express all these functions (Bybee, 2015, see example 2.3). Decategorization refers to the loss of morphosyntactic properties of the source form (Heine, 2003). This means that the construction or one of its parts can become affixes, clitics, or auxiliary verbs. The synthetic future in Romance languages is an example of decategorization because *habēre* lost its independent word status and became an affix (i.e., *cantar-é* 'I will sing') (Bybee, 2015). Erosion means that the grammaticalized form becomes phonetically reduced. For example, the construction *be going to* is often reduced to *gonna* in some cases (Bybee 2003a, 2003b, 2015). It is worth mentioning that these mechanisms are related and tend to occur in order (Heine, 2003). For instance, a construction does not become phonetically reduced without first undergoing semantic bleaching, extension, and decategorization.

(2.2) …que *estan* a las muelas *moliendo* (example taken from Torres Cacoullos, 2012: 78)
…that are at the millis milling (translation taken from Torres Cacoullos, 2012: 78)

Bybee (2003a, 2003b) stated that the frequency of use of these grammaticalized constructions increase as these mechanisms operate because it can be used in more contexts. For instance, the frequency of use of the present progressive increased from Old Spanish to 20th century Spanish (Torres Cacoullos, 2012) as it began to express a progressive aspectual function. Torres Cacoullos (2012) reported that the present progressive experimented an extension of its contexts of use (e.g., locative > non-locative and dynamic verbs > stative verbs), which explains its increased frequency of use.

The grammaticalization mechanisms described earlier are very gradual (Bybee, 2003a, 2015; Bybee et al., 1994; Heine, 2003) and, in most cases, they may take centuries to complete (Hopper & Traugott, 2003). Additionally, these gradual changes are often accompanied by variation in form and function (Bybee, 2003a). Variation can occur within a functional domain in which multiple grams can express similar grammatical functions (Bybee, 2003a; Bybee et al. 1994; Heine, 2003; Schwenter & Torres Cacoullos, 2008). This phenomenon is known as layering. An example of layering can be taken from the Spanish preterit and present perfect because both forms can convey a perfective aspectual function (Burgo, 2010; Copple, 2011; Hernández, 2004, 2008; Holmes & Baluka, 2011; Howe, 2006; Howe & Schwenter, 2008; Jara-Yupanqui & Valenzuela, 2013; Rodríguez-Louro & Jara-Yupanqui, 2011; Schwenter, 1994; Schwenter & Torres Cacoullos, 2008; Serrano, 1996). The fragment in (2.3), taken from Schwenter and Torres Cacoullos (2008), illustrates the present perfect and the preterit expressing the same perfective event. Additionally, variation can occur within given grams because as a gram grammaticalizes, it develops newly grammatical meanings while retaining older functions (Bybee, 2003a; Bybee et al., 1994; Heine, 2003; Schwenter & Torres Cacoullos, 2008). This phenomenon is known as retention. For example, the construction *be going to* presents some degree of retention since it can convey *movement* (2.4a), *intention* (2.4b), or *future* (2.4c) meanings (Bybee, 2003a). Consequently, grammaticalization is a fertile area to investigate language variation and change phenomena.

(2.3) Lo *escuché* esta mañana, lo **he escuchado** esta mañana
(Schwenter & Torres Cacoullos, 2008: 8)
'I heard it this morning, I have heard it this morning'

(2.4) a. We **are going to** Windsor to visit the king. (Bybee, 2003a: 147)

b. We **are going to** get married in June. (Bybee, 2003a: 147)

c. These trees **are going to** lose their leaves. (Bybee, 2003a: 147)

Grammaticalization is possible in part due to two cognitive processes: reanalysis and analogy (Hopper & Traugott, 2003). Reanalysis implies changes in meaning and in syntactic bracketing, while analogy refers to the generalization of a grammatical rule (Hopper & Traugott, 2003). An example of reanalysis and analogy can be presented with the English future construction *be going to*. Figure 2.1 (modified from Hopper & Traugott, 2003: 69) illustrates the different stages in the reanalysis of this construction. According to Hopper and Traugott (2003), in stage I *be going* was interpreted as a unit while *to* was analyzed as part of its argument. In stage II *to* is reanalyzed as part of *be going* and the construction signals future events with direction verbs. In stage III the future construction spreads to other verb classes. The spread of *be going to* to other verb classes is a product of analogy with *will*, since the latter can be used with all verb classes. Finally, stage IV is phonetically reduced to *gonna* since it is reanalyzed as a single morpheme. Consequently, Hopper and Traugott (2003) stated that reanalysis and analogy are an important part of grammaticalization.

In addition, there are some pragmatic factors that come into play during the grammaticalization process. Hopper and Traugott (2003)

Stage I [be going] [to visit Bill]
Stage II [be going to] [visit Bill]
Stage III [be going to] [like Bill]
Stage IV [gonna] [like/visit Bill]

Figure 2.1 Grammaticalization process of the future construction *be going to* (modified from Hopper & Traugott, 2003: 69)

stated that language does not have a will of its own that determines its future. On the contrary, these scholars argued that speakers are a fundamental part of the grammaticalization process since they have intentions which listeners are constantly trying to infer. These intentions and inferences could lead to language change (p.74). Furthermore, they argued that grammaticalization can be considered the result of the continuous negotiation of meaning between the speaker and hearer (p.98). Consequently, this implies that the context in which language takes place (i.e., pragmatic) is a driving force of grammaticalization processes.

According to Hopper and Traugott (2003), the manner in which language context contributes to the grammaticalization process is through the conventionalization of inferences that are frequently generated in certain contexts. According to previous grammaticalization investigations (Hopper & Traugott, 2003; Nicolle, 2012), semantic change may take place when a given construction occurs frequently in a particular context in such a manner that it begins to acquire the meaning or inference expressed in the context. Consequently, this inference can become conventionalized as part of the meaning of the construction (Hopper & Traugott, 2003; Nicolle, 2012). In other words, conversational implicatures (inferences listeners made based on lexical meanings and speech acts) can turn into conventional implicatures (part of the lexical meaning of a construction). For example, Hopper and Traugott (2003) argued that the grammaticalization of *be going to* is due to the conventionalization of the temporal inference developed by *go* as well as the purposive inference associated to *to*.

2.3 Grammaticalization Theory

Grammaticalization Theory proposes hypotheses and predictions about how these language change mechanisms take place. That is, this theory states hypotheses that explain how a lexical item achieves grammatical status, and how it continues to develop further grammatical functions (Bybee et al., 1994; Heine, 2003; Hopper & Traugott, 2003). This theory has found consistent typological correspondences among unrelated languages. For instance, it proposes that different languages use similar lexical sources as grammaticalization material and that these lexical sources follow similar development chains or paths (Bybee, 2015). For example, common lexical material for future forms are *movement to a goal*, *obligation*, and *volition* sources (Bybee, 2015; Bybee et al., 1994). These lexical sources, then, express intention and later future (i.e., prediction), as shown in Figure 2.2 (Bybee, 2015).

Movement to a goal		
Obligation Volition	> Intention	> Future (prediction)

Figure 2.2 Grammaticalization path of the future (Bybee, 2015: 123)

However, Poplack (2011) suggested that each language may follow a different trajectory but arrive at the same outcome (p.224). This scholar contrasted the grammaticalization process of the *go*-verb periphrastic future in French, Brazilian Portuguese, and Spanish. These three languages were selected because they share the similar future variants (synthetic future, periphrastic future, and simple present with a future temporal reference) and these three languages have a common ancestor (i.e., Vulgar Latin). Poplack (2011) found that the factors that conditioned the use of the periphrastic future differed across languages and time periods (19th and 20th centuries). For example, verb class was significant for Spanish in both time periods, but this factor was not selected as significant for French and Brazilian Portuguese. In addition, sentence type was significant for French and Brazilian Portuguese in the 19th century. However, in the 20th century this factor lost its significance in Brazilian Portuguese but was significant for Spanish and French. Consequently, Poplack (2011) stated that the grammaticalization paths of the *go*-verb future markers are not parallel across languages (p.222). Furthermore, this scholar emphasized the importance of incorporating the variationist method into grammaticalization investigations.

The variationist method can be used to examine the degree of grammaticalization using the three lines of evidence: the significance of the effect, the magnitude of the effect, and the direction of the effect (Poplack, 2011; Torres Cacoullos, 2012). This can be done by operationalizing the Grammaticalization Theory hypotheses into different factor groups (Poplack, 2011; Torres Cacoullos, 2012). This means that the variables included in the analysis should reflect Grammaticalization Theory's predictions and hypotheses. The variationist method can be applied to measure the grammaticalization chains or path of a given construction in the diachronic axis. The next section expands on how grammaticalization and the variationist method can be applied in the diachronic axis.

2.4 Grammaticalization in the diachronic axis

It was stated in the previous section that grammaticalization is a very gradual process that may take centuries to complete; consequently, its effects are best seen diachronically (Bybee, 2015; Bybee et al. 1994; Heine, 2003; Hopper & Traugott, 2003). Heine (2003) indicated that this gradual process can be described in three stages (Heine, 2003: 579):

I. A linguistic construction is recruited for grammaticalization
II. The construction acquires a second pattern of use[1] creating ambiguity between the older function and the newer one
III. The initial function of the construction is lost and only the newly acquired function remains

Grammaticalization creates a chain-like structure with an intermediate stage in which a construction can express two (or more) functions (Heine, 2003; Nicolle, 2012). Additionally, during this stage multiple constructions can express similar functions (i.e., layering). For example, in some dialects of Peninsular Spanish the present perfect has acquired a perfective function. This implies that the present perfect expresses a perfect function as well as a perfective one. Additionally, this form coexists with the preterit in the sense that both forms can express perfectiveness (Burgo, 2010; Copple, 2011; Hernández, 2004, 2008; Holmes & Balukas, 2011; Howe, 2006; Howe & Schwenter, 2008; Jara-Yupanqui & Valenzuela Bismarck, 2013; Rodríguez-Louro & Jara-Yupanqui, 2011; Schwenter, 1994; Schwenter & Torres Cacoullos, 2008; Serrano, 1996). This means that the present perfect is in stage II because it may express two functions and it competes with the preterit.

According to Heine (2003), a grammaticalizing construction passes through all the stages of a chain or cline. This point can be illustrated with the compound past (i.e., present perfect, passato prossimo, passé composé, etc.). It has been argued that the grammaticalization chain of the present perfect has four stages (Harris, 1982; Schwenter & Torres Cacoullos, 2008), as shown in Table 2.1. Stage I is characterized by the use of the simple past for all past events. In stage IIa. the compound past is used with past situations ongoing in the present, while the simple past (i.e., preterit, passato remote, passé simple, etc.) is used with most past perfective events. In stage IIb. The present perfect is used to express past iterative events, as documented with Portuguese (Amaral & Howe, 2011, 2012). Amaral & Howe (2011, 2012) stated that in some languages the present perfect may develop an iterative meaning after the resultative stage without going through a persistent past situation (stage IIa.). This entails that the present perfect can pass through either stage IIa. or stage IIb. In stage III the present perfect is used with past situations with current relevance and in stage IV the present perfect is used in all past events (perfect and perfective).

Table 2.1 Grammaticalization chain or cline of the compound past (modified from Schwenter & Torres Cacoullos, 2008: 7)

Stage	Compound past	Simple past
I. Sicilian	Present states resulting from past actions	All past perfectives
IIa. Mexican Spanish, Caribbean Spanish (Delgado-Díaz & Ortiz-López, 2011), some South American Spanish dialects (Harris, 1982)	Past situations still ongoing in the present	Most past perfectives
IIb. Portuguese (Amaral & Howe, 2011, 2012)	Iterative situations extending from past to present	
III. Peninsular Spanish, Catalan	Past situations with current relevance	Past situations without current relevance
IV. French, Northern Italian, Rumanian (Harris, 1982)	All past situations	Formal, written

The variationist method can be applied to track grammaticalization processes in the diachronic axis. Torres Cacoullos (2012) stated that grammaticalization can be observed by comparing the linguistic factors of independent multivariate analyses of different time periods. For instance, Table 2.2 illustrates independent multivariate analyses for the Spanish present progressive with *estar* in three time periods. It can be observed that some factors weakened and others strengthened over time. Additionally, some factors become significant while others lose their significance. For instance, temporal co-occurrence was significant in Old Spanish, but it lost its significance in the 17th and 19th centuries. On the contrary, stativity was not significant in Old Spanish, but it became significant in the 17th and 19th centuries.

2.5 Grammaticalization and the Spanish past forms

This section examines how Grammaticalization Theory and the variationist method can be applied to measure grammaticalization processes of the Spanish past forms. There are several key factors that relate to the Spanish past forms. First, Grammaticalization Theory states that in the diachronic axis newly grammaticalized forms increase their frequency of use while undergoing semantic bleaching (Bybee, 2015; Heine, 2003). Consequently, if a past form is grammaticalizing it is expected to find an increase in frequency and weakening of some linguistic constraint

Table 2.2 Multivariate analysis of the factors that predict the use of the present progressive with *estar* in Old Spanish, 17th century and 19th century (modified from Torres Cacoullos, 2012: 93)

			Old Spanish	17th century	19th century
Factor		N	119/745 (16%)	180/1013 (18%)	317/1460 (22%)
			Factor weight	Factor weight	Factor weight
Aspect	Limited duration		.68	.72	.73
	Extended duration		.32	.17	.15
	Range		32	55	58
Locative co-occurrence	Present		.77	.74	.62
	Absent		.48	.48	.49
	Range		29	26	13
Polarity	Affirmative declarative		.55	.57	.58
	Negative, interrogative		.31	.21	.2
	Range		24	36	38
Temporal co-occurrence	Present		.70	[.54]	[.57]
	Absent		.47	[.49]	[.49]
	Range		23		
Stativity	Dynamic predicate		[.50]	.56	.58
	Stative predicate		[.49]	.36	.32
	Range			20	26

Not significant factors showed with []

diachronically. For instance, it is expected that the imperfect progressive with *estar* loses its locative meaning through time, following Torres Cacoullos' (2000, 2012, 2015) results on the present progressive with *estar*. This hypothesis is based on the fact that the imperfect progressive with *estar*, as well as its present counterpart, emerged from a locative construction (Bybee et al., 1994; Bybee and Torres Cacoullos, 2009; Torres Cacoullos, 2000, 2015).

Additionally, it can be expected to find that some linguistic constraints strengthen over time, because during the grammaticalization process a construction can acquire new semantic or pragmatic functions. For example, Copple (2011) investigated the perfect-to-perfective grammaticalization of the Spanish present perfect in the diachronic dimension. This scholar studied the use of the present perfect in three different time periods (15th, 17th, and 19th centuries). It is worth highlighting that among her findings the factor temporal reference strengthened over time. The present perfect was favored by very recent and irrelevant temporal references in the 15th century. This form then spread to indeterminate temporal references in the 17th century. Finally, in the 19th century the present perfect extended to hodiernal (today) temporal references. Copple's (2011) data shows how this aspectual form acquired new functions over time by extending its temporal reference from very recent and irrelevant contexts to indeterminate, and later hodiernal temporal contexts.

The concepts of layering and retention are important when studying Spanish past forms because they deal with variation across different constructions and within a specific construction (Bybee et al. 1994; Hopper & Traugott, 2003; Heine, 2003; Schwenter & Torres Cacoullos, 2008). This implies that there would be variation between newly grammaticalized constructions with older ones.

It is worth mentioning that most of the Spanish past forms have not been investigated under a grammaticalization perspective which makes it difficult to determine which ones are grammaticalizing. For example, the preterit and imperfect are regarded as stable and non-variable forms. In other words, researchers assume that the preterit always expresses perfectivity and the imperfect always conveys imperfectivity (i.e., form-function symmetry assumption) (e.g., Cuza, 2010; Domínguez, Arche & Myles, 2010; Montrul, 2002; Montrul & Slabakova, 2000; Salaberry, 2003; Slabakova & Montrul, 1999, among many others). As a result, these forms have not been widely studied under a grammaticalization perspective (Delgado-Díaz, 2018a). Consequently, it is unknown if the preterit and imperfect's linguistic constraints changed through time.

Regarding the past progressives, these constructions are newer since they are not inherited from Latin (Penny, 2000) and periphrastic constructions tend to be less grammaticalized and, as consequence, are usually in earlier grammaticalization stage (Bybee, 2015; Bybee et al., 1994). This point is important because "periphrastic constructions tend to replace morphological ones over time" (Hopper & Traugott, 2003: 9). This has two fundamental implications: first, the past progressive forms may be grammaticalizing and they may variate with other past forms. Second, the emergence of the progressive forms may cause the Spanish aspectual system to shift since these forms may compete or even replace the simple ones (Hopper & Traugott, 2003).

It is worth mentioning that Bybee and Torres Cacoullos (2009) constructed a grammaticalization index for the present progressive with *estar*, which included the locative co-occurrence, adjacency (i.e., intervening material between the auxiliary verb and the -ndo form), association (i.e., number of -ndo forms associated to one auxiliary verb), and fusion (i.e., position of the clitic). Bybee and Torres Cacoullos (2009) and Torres Cacoullos (2011, 2012) stated that these factors correlate to the grammaticalization stage of the Spanish progressive construction. Recall that this construction originated from a locative source that meant to be located in a place performing an action (Bybee et al., 1994; Torres Cacoullos, 2000, 2015). The fragment in (2.6), taken from Torres Cacoullos (2015), illustrates a use of the present progressive from the 13th century that co-occurred with a locative construction *aqui* 'here'. Co-occurrence with locative constructions is important because Grammaticalization Theory states that locative constructions are a common cross-linguistic source for progressive grams (Bybee et al., 1994). However, the locative meaning is weakened and is eventually lost through time (Bybee et al., 1994). Bybee and Torres Cacoullos (2009) and Torres Cacoullos (2000, 2012) demonstrated that the development of the Spanish present progressive encompasses the weakening and eventual loss of its original locative meaning.

(2.6) u<uestr>os hebreos **estan** aqui ***razonando***. (Torres Cacoullos, 2015: 3)
Your Hebrews are here conferring. (Translation taken from Torres Cacoullos, 2015: 3)

Regarding adjacency, this factor measures the intervening material between the auxiliary verb and the -ndo form. For instance, the fragment in (2.7) illustrates an instance of the present progressive in *La Celestina* (taken from Bybee & Torres Cacoullos, 2009: 202). This example shows that the phrase *Melibea muy afligida* 'Melibea very distressed' appears between *estar* and the -ndo form. According to Bybee and Torres Cacoullos (2009), as the present progressive grammaticalizes it tends to appear less with intervening material because the auxiliary verb and the -ndo are viewed as a single unit.

(2.7) ***Está*** Melibea muy afligida ***hablando*** con Lucrecia sobre la tardaça de Calisto. (Bybee & Torres Cacoullos, 2009: 202)
Melibea is very distressed talking with Lucrecia about Calisto's tardiness. (Translation taken from Bybee & Torres Cacoullos, 2009: 202)

The next factor that Bybee and Torres Cacoullos (2009) analyze is association, which relates to the number of -ndo forms that can be associated to one auxiliary verb. The example in (2.8), taken from Bybee and Torres Cacoullos (2009), illustrates a use of *ir* (yvan) 'to go' with two -ndo forms associated to it. However, according to these scholars, as the present progressive grammaticalizes it tends to appear with one -ndo form because the unit-hood of the present progressive is composed of an auxiliary verb and a single -ndo form.

(2.8) le *yvan menguando* los bastimentos e *creciendo* las necesidades.
(Bybee & Torres Cacoullos, 2009: 202)
The supplies were diminishing and the necessities growing.

The final factor included by Bybee and Torres Cacoullos (2009) is fusion, which refers to the position of the clitics. According to these scholars, the use of the clitic before the auxiliary verb correlates with higher levels of unit-hood in progressive constructions. They based this hypothesis on the fact that verbs or highly grammaticalized constructions do not accept the clitic attached to them, as in *veolo* 'I see him/it' or *he vistolo* 'I have seen him/it'. Consequently, they argue that *los fueron conservando* 'they were preserving them' in (2.9) is as much as a single unit as *los convervan* 'they preserve them'.

(2.9) otros, que tuvieron principios grandes, y *los fueron conservando* y *los* conservan y mantienen en el ser que comenzaron. (Bybee & Torres Cacoullos, 2009: 202)
other, that had great beginnings, and they were conserving them and they conserve and maintain them as they began.

The Spanish present progressive with *estar* appears to be in an advanced grammaticalization stage because Bybee and Torres Cacoullos (2009) found that the grammaticalization index increased diachronically. In addition, this construction has grammaticalized further grammatical functions because it may also express habituality and future events (Aponte-Alequín & Ortiz-López, 2010; Claes & Ortiz-López, 2011; Cortés-Torres, 2005). Consequently, the grammaticalization index proposed by Bybee and Torres Cacoullos' (2009) may provide an insight of the Spanish past progressives because of the similarities between the present and past progressives (imperfect progressive and preterit progressive) since both forms emerged from a locative source, they are periphrastic constructions, and they use the same auxiliary verb (mainly *estar*). Therefore, it is possible that these factors apply to the imperfect progressive and preterit progressive. However, Torres Cacoullos (personal communication) stated that the past forms usually lag behind present ones. This means that the past progressive may not be as grammaticalized as the present progressive.

2.6 Conclusions

This chapter examined the main mechanisms and hypotheses proposed by Grammaticalization Theory. Additionally, it was added, that the variationist method can be applied to grammaticalization investigations (Poplack, 2011; Torres Cacoullos, 2012). It was mentioned that the variationist method can help track grammaticalization changes through time, determine the grammaticalization stage of a construction, determine a prototypical meaning of a form (Díaz-Campos, Galarza, & Delgado-Díaz, 2016), and account for diachronic variation. This chapter also discussed how grammaticalization and the variationist method can be applied to investigate the Spanish past forms, which could be done by incorporating Grammaticalization Theory hypotheses. Finally, special attention was given to Bybee and Torres Cacoullos' (2009) grammaticalization index because it can be used to track the grammaticalization processes of the past progressive constructions. In addition, Bybee and Torres Cacoullos' (2009) results of the present progressive can be used as a comparison for the past progressives. More specifically, it can reveal the grammaticalization order of Spanish progressive constructions.

Note

1 Heine (2003: 579) mentions that the constructions acquires a second function but there are cases in which the constructions may acquire more functions. For example, the present progressive may express progressiveness, habituality, and future events in Puerto Rican Spanish (Aponte-Alequín & Ortiz-López, 2010; Claes & Ortiz-López, 2011; Cortés-Torres, 2005).

3 Previous studies on Spanish past forms

3.1 Introduction

This chapter examines previous investigations on Spanish tense and aspect. More specifically, it focuses on studies which analyzed the preterit, imperfect, present perfect, preterit progressive, and imperfect progressive. Due to the multiple forms analyzed, this chapter presents a brief overview of previous studies focusing on aspectual function, lexical semantics, and discourse functions[1]. These are the main factors that are said to influence the choice between these past forms. The last part of this chapter attempts to identify gaps in the previous research as well as develop an aspectual map of the past forms based on previous investigations. The goal of the aspectual map is to demonstrate that each form can express more than one aspectual function. Ultimately, this will allow arguing against studying these forms in binary categorizations (i.e., preterit vs imperfect, imperfect vs imperfect progressive, preterit vs present perfect, etc.) and it will also demonstrate that the Spanish past aspectual system is full of neutralized contexts (Poplack, 2018).

3.2 The preterit

3.2.1 Aspectual function

Traditionally, the preterit is associated with a perfective function (Alcina Franch & Blecua, 1975; Bello, 1847; Serrano, 2006; RAE, 1973; Westfall, 1995, 2003). Recall that the perfective views the event as completed (Comrie, 1976) or temporally bounded (Bybee et al., 1994; Salas-González, 1998). This means that *leyó*, in example (3.1), is interpreted as a completed event in the past. There have been substantial investigations that argue that the preterit entails a perfective reading (Baker & Quesada, 2011; Delgado-Díaz, in press; Howe & Schwenter,

2008; Schwenter & Torres Cacoullos, 2008; RAE, 1973, 2010; Westfall, 1995, 2003, among others).

(3.1) Juan *leyó* el libro.
       Juan read the book.

However, there are investigations that attribute other aspectual functions to the preterit. This form has been reported to express a perfect function in Río Platense Spanish (Henderson, 2010; Menegotto, 2008; Ocampo, 2008; Rodríguez-Louro, 2009, 2010), Chilean, Paraguayan, Uruguayan Spanish (Henderson, 2010), Puerto Rican, and Dominican Spanish (Delgado-Díaz & Ortiz-López, 2011). However, this function is not discussed further because perfect aspectual function falls outside the scope of this investigation.

Some scholars have argued that the preterit can express habitual events (Ayres, 2009; Delgado-Díaz, in press; Cipria & Roberts, 2000). Cipria and Roberts (2000) argued that the sentence in (3.2) can be interpreted as 3,000 liters of oil flowed through the pipes daily. This may indicate that the preterit can have a habitual interpretation.

(3.2) *Corrieron* 3000 litros de petróleo por las cañerías. (Cipria & Roberts, 2000: 7)
       3000 liters of oil flowed through the pipes. (Translation taken from Cipria & Roberts, 2000: 7)

Cipria and Roberts (2000) stated that in cases, such as the one in (3.2), the alternation between the preterit and imperfect is "pragmatically motivated" (p.8). However, these scholars do not clearly explain these pragmatic mechanisms that alter the interpretation of the preterit. It could be inferred that in some contexts the preterit neutralizes with the imperfect within discourse, according to Neutralization in Discourse Hypothesis (Sankoff, 1988). Consequently, it could be argued that the preterit can serve the same function as the imperfect presenting instances of form-function asymmetry (Poplack, 2018).

Other researchers have argued that the preterit can also express a progressive aspectual function (Brucart, 2003; Champion, 1973). For instance, Champion (1973) argued that previous theoretical accounts have stated that the preterit presents the situation as a whole: beginning, middle, and end (i.e., perfective). This scholar argued that this view is too simplistic and does not account for all the functions it can fulfill. Furthermore, he added that the preterit can present an event without a beginning or an end. For example, *funcionó* 'worked' in (3.3) has a progressive meaning because it denotes that the machine is still working.

(3.3) Reparó la máquina y después *funcionó* bien. (Champion, 1973: 1043)
S/he repaired the machine and then it worked well.

Similarly, Brucart (2003) argued that the preterit can be used in progressive contexts. The sentence in (3.4a) illustrates a preterit modified by a progressive adverb *durante* 'for'. According to this scholar, the preterit in example (3.4a) has a completed interpretation, while the imperfect in (3.4b) may entail that the subject still studies English in the university. This means that the difference between the preterit and imperfect is a completed and non-completed interpretation. However, this distinction is problematic since both the preterit and imperfect can be interpreted as completed (i.e., the subject does not study English in the present). In other words, Brucart (2003) makes a form-function symmetry assumption. On the contrary, a present construction (simple present, present progressive, etc.) should be required to express that the subject is still studying English. The important aspect of Brucart's (2003) study is that the preterit can be used to express a progressive function and it can neutralize with the imperfect.

(3.4) a. Durante tres años *estudié* inglés en la Universidad. (Brucart, 2003: 3)
For three years, I studied English in the University.
b. En aquel momento *estudiaba* inglés en la Universidad. (Brucart, 2003: 3)
In that moment, I was studying/studied English in the University.

However, Champion (1973) and Brucart (2003) did not include quantitative analyses. Consequently, it is difficult to determine the frequency of use of the preterit with a progressive function. In addition, their analyses do not allow determining the linguistic and extra-linguistic factors that predict the use of the preterit in this context. However, recent investigations have studied this phenomenon with quantitative analyses.

For instance, Ayres (2009) investigated the use of past forms (i.e., preterit, imperfect, and imperfect progressive) in Houston Spanish and Mexican Spanish (Cuernavaca, Morelos, and Polotitlán) from a variationist perspective. The participants were 45 speakers of Mexican descent living in Houston, Texas and 12 Spanish monolinguals living in

Mexico, as a comparison group. The participants were divided by age, sex, and generation in the U.S. (first, second, and third generation). Ayres (2009) coded for the following linguistic variables: grammatical person (first, second, and third), number (singular and plural)[2], aspect (perfective and imperfective), type of verb (stative and non-stative), style (informal/spoken and formal/written), and form of the imperfect (progressive and simple). This researcher also included the following extra-linguistic variables: age (young 18–29, adults, 30–50, and older 51+), sex, generation (first, second, and third), and level of English (native, near-native, good knowledge of English, some knowledge of English, and very little knowledge of English).

Regarding the preterit, Ayres (2009) found that this form is commonly used to express perfectivity by all generations, with more than 90% frequency of use. However, Ayres (2009) found that the preterit was also used to express imperfectivity. An example of the preterit in a habitual context is presented in (3.5). The participant is talking about a habitual event in which s/he used to translate the news. However, the participant used the preterit *insitió* 'insisted' in this context.

(3.5) …y mi abuela me sentaba en frente de la televisión para que yo le tradujera los noticieros. O sea, que ***insistió*** que tradujera los noticieros. (Ayres, 2009: 165)
…and my grandmother used to sit me in front of the television so that I could translate the news to her. I mean, she insisted that I translated the news.

The rate of the preterit with imperfective meaning increased according to the generation. The contras group had a rate of 1.5%, the first generation had a 2.0% rate, the second generation had a usage rate of 5.9%, and third generation had a rate of 7.7% in the short sociolinguistic interview. Ayres (2009) performed an ANOVA which found that these groups differed significantly. This researcher concludes that there is an ongoing change in the Spanish of Houston because the third generation was statistically different from the contrast group. In addition, she discards the possibility that this aspectual change occurs in non-contact situations because of the low frequency of the use of the preterit with imperfective meaning (pp.246–247). Therefore, Ayres (2009) attributed these aspectual changes to contact with English.

However, there are two main issues with Ayres' (2009) study: first, this scholar rejects the notion that the preterit in imperfectivity contexts does not occur in Mexico Spanish. However, this group used the preterit in perfectivity contexts with a rate of 1.7%. This may indicate that this variation originated in Mexican Spanish and it may be subject to contact accelerated language change. Second, Ayres (2009) based her conclusion on results from ANOVAs. However, this scholar does not explain why ANOVAs were performed with nominal variables. This type of statistical analysis is best suited for continuous variables (Larson-Hall, 2010). Consequently, ANOVAs may be inappropriate for the type of variable in this investigation and may cause type I errors.

Delgado-Díaz (in press) also found that the preterit was used to express habituality and progressiveness in Puerto Rican Spanish. This scholar investigated the use of different past forms to identify the aspectual functions that they could express. There were 33 participants from Puerto Rico, who were all living in Puerto Rico. The data was obtained with sociolinguistic interviews, which included questions eliciting habitual, progressive, and perfective events. The results indicate that the preterit was mainly used to express a perfective function: 1,650 cases (89.9%). Additionally, Delgado-Díaz (in press) found limited uses of this form conveyed a habitual function: nine cases (.5%), and a progressive function: 42 cases (2.5%). These results suggest that the preterit is used more frequently to express a progressive function than a habitual one.

Additionally, some SLA studies have documented the preterit with a progressive aspectual function in Spanish native speakers (Baker & Quesada, 2011; Cuza, 2010; Domínguez et al., 2010). For instance, Baker and Quesada (2011) investigated the effect of adverbial cues in the acquisition of Spanish preterit and imperfect. The participants for this study were 30 learners (ten beginners, ten intermediate, and ten advanced) and ten native speakers as a comparison group. The participants completed two cloze tasks: one with adverbial cues and another task without adverbial modifications. Among their results, it is important to highlight that they found a lot of variability within the Spanish native speakers. For instance, Baker and Quesada (2011) expected the use of the imperfect in sentence (3.6) because there are two events occurring at the same time. However, Spanish native speakers used the preterit and imperfect at a 50% rate. This finding suggests that the preterit can be used in ongoing contexts and these forms can be neutralized (Delgado-Díaz, in press; Poplack, 2018).

(3.6) Mi amigo es artista, así que él (*examinaba/examinó*) la pintura con interés pero yo, como escritor, (*leía/leí*) una novela. (Baker & Quesada, 2011: 10)
My friend is an artist, so he was examining/examined the painting with interest but I, as a writer, was reading/read a novel. (Translation taken from Baker & Quesada, 2011: 10)

3.2.2 Lexical aspect

The preterit is commonly associated with accomplishment and achievement verbs because these types of verbs have an inherit end point (i.e., telic) (Acero, 1990; Alcina Franch & Blecua, 1975; Cipria & Roberts, 2000; RAE, 1973, 2010; Westfall, 1995), following the predictions of the Lexical Aspect Hypothesis (Andersen & Shirai, 1996). However, this does not entail that the preterit cannot be used with state and activity verbs. For instance, Cipria and Roberts (2000) stated that the preterit in (3.7) can have an atelic reading. This implies that *corrió* 'ran' can be interpreted as an activity verb because it does not have an inherent end point.

(3.7) *Corrió* petróleo por las cañerías. (Cipria & Roberts, 2000: 7)
Oil flowed through the pipes. (Translation taken from Cipria & Roberts, 2000: 7)

Similarly, Westfall (1995) argued that the preterit can be used with atelic verbs. This scholar investigated different Spanish past forms (preterit, imperfect, imperfect progressive, and preterit progressive) under a generative perspective. She found that the preterit can be used with activity, states, accomplishments, and achievement verbs. However, the interpretation of the event is altered according to the lexical semantics. Consequently, the preterit focuses on the initial and end point of the event with activities and accomplishments. The example in (3.8) illustrates a use of the preterit with an activity verb *compitió* 'she competed'. Westfall (1995) argued that the preterit with stative verbs is complex because it can be interpreted as inchoative or bounded states. Inchoative interpretations focus on the initiative phase of the event, as illustrated in (3.9), while bounded states refer to the whole duration of the event, as depicted in (3.10).

(3.8) Entonces, cuando yo nací, mi mamá ya era clavadista. Eh.- durante el lapso entre el nacimiento de mi hermano mayor y yo, mi mamá *compitió*, y posteriormente a mi nacimiento, siguió compitiendo. (Westfall, 1995: 163–164)
So, when I was born, my mom was already a diver...uh...during the gap between my older brother's birth and my own, my mom competed and after my birth she continued to compete. (Translation taken from Westfall, 1995: 164)

(3.9) Mis padres *se conocieron* en el colegio. (Westfall, 1995: 170)
My parents met in high school. (Translation taken from Westfall, 1995: 170)

(3.10) *Viví* dos años en España. (Westfall, 1995: 171)
I lived in Spain for two years. (Translation taken from Westfall, 1995: 171)

Recent investigations have analyzed the preterit in Spanish native speakers using a variationist methodology (Delgado-Díaz, 2014, 2018b; Rojas, 2015). These studies are important for two main reasons: first, they found evidence that supports the Lexical Aspect Hypothesis (Andersen & Shirai, 1996), as well as previous theoretical accounts (Acero, 1990, Alcina Franch & Blecua, 1975, RAE, 1973, 2010). Generally, these investigations have found that the preterit is favored by accomplishment and achievement verbs (Delgado-Díaz, 2014, 2018b; Rojas, 2015). Second, Delgado-Díaz' (2014, 2018b) investigations show that the preterit is not used exclusively with accomplishment and achievement verbs. Rather, it can appear with states (3.11) and activity verbs (3.12) with a lower frequency of use. For example, Delgado-Díaz (2014) found that the preterit was used 25% of the time with activity verbs and 28.7% with stative verbs. These results support the notion that lexical semantics is probabilistic (Bardovi-Harlig, 2000). This means that the preterit tends to appear more frequently with accomplishment and achievement verbs, but it can also be used less frequently with state and activity verbs.

(3.11) de Hugo para acá *fueron* los peores. (SJ031022H96) (Delgado-Díaz, 2014: 30)
Since (Hurricane) Hugo until now there were the worst.

(3.12) fue su amigo secreto quién le *hizo* las maldades. (SJ06032M96) (Delgado-Díaz, 2014: 30)
It was his/her secret friend who did him/her childish pranks.

It is worth mentioning that Delgado-Díaz' (2014, 2018b) and Rojas' (2015) studies also uncovered nuances regarding the semantic classes that favor the use of the preterit. For instance, Delgado-Díaz (2014, 2018b) found that the preterit is slightly disfavored by accomplishment verbs in Puerto Rican Spanish. This scholar argued that the Puerto Rican Spanish is sensitive to duration making the preterit less compatible with accomplishment verbs. Additionally, Rojas (2015) suggests that the preterit is favored by activity verbs in U.S. Mexican Spanish. However, this researcher does not explain this finding. The results from Delgado-Díaz' (2014, 2018b) and Rojas' (2015) investigations suggest that the preterit is susceptible to language variation and change.

3.2.3 Discourse functions

In terms of discourse factors that influence the use of the preterit, previous investigations have stated that this form is mainly used to express foreground information (Bardovi-Harlig, 2000; Delgado-Díaz, 2018b; Silva-Corvalán, 1983; Weinrich, 1968; Westfall, 1995) as predicted by the Discourse Hypothesis (Hopper, 1979). Recall that foreground information is temporally anchored and is essential to a narrative because it moves the events forward in chronological order (Hopper, 1979). For instance, Westfall (1995) provides an example with a series of preterits expressing foreground information (3.13). The verbs *cociné* 'I cooked', *limpié* 'I cleaned', *miré* 'I watched', and *leí* 'I read' move the narrative forward and present the events in chronological order.

(3.13) Anoche, *cociné*, *limpié* un poco, *miré* la televisión, y *leí* un par de horas. (Westfall, 1995: 195)
Last night I cooked, I cleaned a little, I watched television, and I read a couple of hours. (Translation taken from Westfall, 1995: 195)

There are several quantitative investigations that have studied the preterit and its discourse function (Delgado-Díaz, 2014, 2018b, Silva-Corvalán, 1983). For instance, Silva-Corvalán (1983) investigated the distribution of different Spanish tense and aspect forms in oral narratives of 27 Chilean and three Mexican Spanish speakers. The main goal of this investigation was to delimit the meanings of the present and past progressive and non-progressive forms during discourse. According to Silva-Corvalán (1983), each form has a specific meaning that determines its use in discourse. This scholar added that there may be overlapping functions between some forms; however, this overlapping does not occur in narratives because "…form-specific content become evident blocking the possibility of replacing a form, and at the same time retaining the speaker's communicative intent" (Silva-Corvalán, 1983: 761). This implies that variation does not occur within discourse. The results support the Discourse Hypothesis because the preterit was used more frequently (76%) in the resolution-coda part of the narrative, which is associated with foreground information. However, Silva-Corvalán (1983) found that there were limited cases (5%[3]) in which the preterit was used to express background information. These results suggest that the preterit is not categorically to express foreground information and that there is variation within discourse, contrary to Silva-Corvalán's (1983) statement.

Delgado-Díaz (2018b) also examined the role of the type of discourse in his investigation, which studied the use of the preterit and imperfect in Buenos Aires and Puerto Rican Spanish. The results indicate that discourse function (foreground vs background) was a significant predictor in Buenos Aires Spanish. The preterit was favored by foreground information (p=.55). On the contrary, discourse function was not significant in Puerto Rican Spanish. Additionally, this investigation found that the preterit can be used to express background information. This scholar found that the preterit was used 22.7% of the time to express background information in Buenos Aires Spanish. These findings suggest that the preterit is susceptible to dialectal variation. More specifically, it appears that discourse function does not operate in all Spanish dialects. Additionally, these results support the notion that the Discourse Hypothesis (Hopper, 1979) is probabilistic (Bardovi-Harlig, 2000).

3.2.4 Summary of the preterit

This section examined previous investigations regarding the preterit emphasizing on the aspectual functions it can express, its lexical semantic restrictions, and the discourse functions it can convey. Regarding the aspectual meaning, it was found that the preterit can convey perfectivity, habituality (Cipria & Roberts, 2000; Delgado-Díaz, in press), progressiveness (Brucart, 2003; Delgado-Díaz, in press), and perfect events (Henderson, 2010; Menegotto, 2008; Ocampo, 2008; Rodríguez-Louro, 2009). This suggests that the preterit expresses a wide range of aspectual meanings. However, Delgado-Díaz' (in press) study suggests that the cases in which the preterit can convey progressiveness and habituality are limited.

Regarding the lexical semantics associated with the preterit, this review found that most theoretical studies argue that the preterit is used with accomplishment and achievement verbs (Acero, 1990; Alcina Franch & Blecua, 1975; RAE, 1973, 2010). However, other generative accounts argued that it can be used to express atelic events (Cipria & Roberts, 2000, Westfall, 1995). Moreover, Westfall (1995) stated that the preterit can be used with activity, stative, accomplishment, and achievement verbs. Delgado-Díaz' (2014, 2018b) and Rojas' (2015) investigations contributed to this debate by performing quantitative analyses. These studies found that the preterit can be used with all the lexical semantic classes, but less frequently with activities and states. These findings support the notion that the Lexical Aspect Hypothesis' predictions are probabilistic (Bardovi-Harlig, 2000). Additionally, Delgado-Díaz (2014, 2018b) and Rojas documented nuances regarding the preterit's lexical semantic restrictions. For instance, Delgado-Díaz (2014, 2018b) found that accomplishment verbs were slightly disfavored by the preterit in Puerto Rican Spanish. Additionally, Rojas (2015) suggests that activity verbs may favor the use of the preterit. This implies that the lexical semantic associated with the preterit may be susceptible to language variation and change, which presents a fertile area of research from a diachronic perspective.

Finally, this section reviewed investigations that considered the discourse functions associated with the preterit. Previous accounts have found that this form is used to express foreground information (Delgado-Díaz, 2018b; Silva-Corvalán, 1983; Westfall, 1995), following the Discourse Hypothesis (Hopper, 1979). However, this discussion showed that the preterit is not used categorically with foreground information since it can be used less frequently to express background information (Delgado-Díaz, 2018b; Silva-Corvalán, 1983). Additionally, Delgado-Díaz (2018b) found that this factor was not significant in Puerto Rican Spanish, which suggests that type of information does not operate in all Spanish dialects. Furthermore, this survey also supports the notion that discourse function is probabilistic (Bardovi-Harlig, 2000), as in the case of lexical semantics. Finally, previous studies suggest that narratives provide contexts in which variation may occur, contrary to Silva-Corvalán's (1983) claim.

3.3 The imperfect

3.3.1 Aspectual function

The imperfect is commonly associated with habitual and progressive aspectual functions (Ayres, 2009; Baker & Quesada, 2011; Bello, 1847; Bybee et al., 1994; Cipria & Roberts, 2000; Comrie, 1976; Delgado-Díaz, in press; Lamanna, 2008, 2012; Montrul & Slabakova, 2003; RAE, 1973, 2010; Rodríguez-Ramalle, 2005). Recall that progressiveness is defined as a dynamic event that unfolds within a specific time frame (Comrie, 1976), while habituality is defined as an event that is repeated during an extensive period of time in such a manner that it becomes an inherent characteristic of that event (Comrie, 1976).

However, there is evidence of the imperfect expressing a perfective aspectual function (Ayres, 2009; Baker & Quesda, 2011; Delgado-Díaz, in press; Doiz, 2011; Rodriguez, 2004; Silva-Corvalán, 1994; Zentella, 1997). Some of these studies argue that the imperfect is used to express a perfective aspectual function in language contact situations (Ayres, 2009; Silva-Corvalán, 1994; Zentella, 1997). Silva-Corvalán (1994) and

Zentella (1997) argue that Spanish in contact with English causes heritage speakers to neutralize the preterit and imperfect distinction with stative verbs, as illustrated in (3.14).

(3.14) Yo *estaba* en esa escuela hasta el séptimo grado. (Zentella, 1997: 187)
I was in that school until the seventh grade. (Translation taken from Zentella, 1997: 187)

Nevertheless, the imperfect with a perfective function have been documented in non-contact Spanish (Ayres, 2009; Baker & Quesada, 2011; Doiz, 2011; Rodíguez, 2004). Rodríguez (2004) argued that the imperfect can be used to express a perfective function with telic events, as illustrated in (3.15). This scholar stated that the use of the imperfect entails a perfective event that lasted the entire time interval. Additionally, the imperfect with a perfective function can be used with a property reading (the verb expresses a property associated generally with the subject, Doiz, 2011), as presented in (3.16). Doiz (2011) explained that the imperfect in (3.16) presents the situation as a whole (i.e., perfective), but the speaker chooses the imperfect to highlight that it was hot all year. It is worth noticing that these investigations do not include a quantitative analysis, which makes it difficult to determine the frequency of use of the imperfect with a perfective aspectual function.

(3.15) Ayer Borges *moría* en Ginebra. (Rodríguez, 2004: 99)
Yesterday Borges was dying in Geneva. (Translation taken from Rodríguez, 2004: 99)

(3.16) El año pasado en París *hacía* calor. (Doiz, 2011: 66)
It was hot last year in Paris. (Translation taken from Doiz, 2011: 66)

There are some studies that provide an insight into the frequency of use of the imperfect with a perfective function (Ayres, 2009; Baker & Quesada, 2011; Delgado-Díaz, in press). For instance, Ayres (2009) found that Spanish native speakers from Cuernavaca, Morelos, Polotitlán, and Querétaro used the imperfect in perfective contexts with a rate of 1.7%. Ayres coded *empezaba* 'I started' in (3.17) as perfective because the speaker is talking about the first time that he started learning English. Baker and Quesada (2011) found that Spanish native speakers used the imperfect 80% of the time in (3.18), while Baker and Quesada (2011) expected the preterit since it '…reflects on a recently completed action' (p.10).

(3.17)   Y así fue que empecé. Empecé y, claro, ya teniendo, este, la fundación en... ¿Cómo se diría? Umm, en español, hice traslado al inglés yo sin saberlo. Pero ya después ya que veía las palabras y las veía por escrito, decía yo "esto no es feerst, tiene que ser first porque así es que ellos lo dicen, pues". Entonces así *empezaba* yo. (Ayres, 2009: 111)
And that was how I started. I started, of course, already having, I mean, a foundation in...How should it be said? Ummm in Spanish, I made the transition to English without knowing it. But after I used to see the words and I saw them written, I would say this is not 'feerst', this must to be 'first' because that is how they say it. That is how I started.

(3.18)   ...que me comí un plato entero de espaguetis. ¡(*Estaba/Estuvo*) riquísimo! (Baker & Quesada, 2011: 10)
...that I ate a whole plate of spaghetti. It was/was delicious! (Translation taken from Baker & Quesada, 2011: 10)

Delgado-Díaz (in press) also documented the imperfect in perfective contexts. Recall that this scholar studied the aspectual function of different past forms. Regarding the imperfect, the results indicate that this form was mainly used to express progressiveness (1,413 cases (55.5%)) and habituality (716 cases (28.1%)). There were limited cases of the imperfect with a perfective function (21 cases (.8%)). Consequently, Delgado-Díaz (in press) argued that the imperfect's main functions are progressiveness and habituality, but it can express perfectiveness in limited cases.

3.3.2 Lexical semantics

Most studies on the imperfect have stated that the lexical semantic plays a significant role with respect to its use. Several theoretical (Acero, 1990; Alcina Franch & Blecua, 1975; Cipria & Roberts, 2000; RAE, 1973, 2010; Westfall, 1995), second language acquisition (Bardovi-Harlig, 2000; Delgado-Díaz & Ortiz-López, 2012; Montrul, 2002; Montrul & Slabakova, 2003; Salaberry, 2003; among others), and variationist investigations (Delgado-Díaz, 2014, 2018b; Rojas, 2015) have found evidence that indicate that the imperfect is associated with state and activity verbs, as predicted by the Lexical Aspect Hypothesis (Andersen & Shirai, 1996). Recall that the imperfect is compatible with states and activities because they are durative and atelic.

However, some investigations have found that the imperfect can be used with other semantic classes as well (Delgado-Díaz, 2014, 2018b;

Westfall, 1995). For instance, Westfall (1995) investigated the lexical semantic restrictions of the imperfect from a generative perspective. This analysis found that the imperfect can be used with accomplishment and achievement verbs. According to this scholar, the imperfect with accomplishment verbs focuses on the internal structure of an event. Consequently, *comía* 'was eating' in (3.19) focuses on the event of eating an apple without including its end point. Similarly, the imperfect can be used with achievement verbs to signal the preliminary stage of a single event (Westfall, 1995: 227). This implies that *se convertía* 'it was changing' in (3.20) indicates the beginning of the event. However, Westfall (1995) noted that the imperfect has some restriction with achievement verbs. For example, the imperfect cannot be used with verbs such as *estrellarse* 'to crash' because it cannot be associated with phases leading to the event. According to this analysis, the sentence in (3.21) would be ungrammatical. However, this example is problematic since *se estrellaba* 'was crashing' can be interpreted as an ongoing process. Additionally, the imperfect can provide a slow-motion effect to the event.

(3.19) **Comía** una manzana cuando lo vi. (Westfall, 1995: 226)
He was eating an apple when I saw him. (Translation taken from Westfall, 1995: 226)

(3.20) La lluvia *se convertía* en briza (Westfall, 1995: 226)
The rain was changing into a breeze. (Translation taken from Westfall, 1995: 226)

(3.21) *El avión *se estrellaba*. (Westfall, 1995: 227)
*The plane was crashing. (Translation taken from Westfall, 1995: 227)

Other studies have investigated the imperfect from a variationist perspective, and have found that the imperfect may have other tendencies (Delgado-Díaz, 2014, 2018b; Rojas, 2015). For instance, Delgado-Díaz (2014, 2018b) found that the imperfect was favored by accomplishment verbs in Puerto Rican Spanish. This scholar suggested that speakers are sensitive to the duration of the verb since the imperfect is favored by durative verb classes (i.e., states, activities, and accomplishments). Additionally, Rojas (2015) found that the imperfect was not favored by activity verbs. Unfortunately, Rojas (2015) did not address this finding making it difficult to explain its implications. These results suggest that the imperfect's lexical semantic restrictions do not function similarly in all Spanish dialects.

3.3.3 Discourse functions

The imperfect is commonly associated with background information (Delgado-Díaz, 2018b; Gonzales, 1995; Gutiérrez-Araus, 1998; Reyes, 1990; Silva-Corvalán, 1983; Soto, 2011; Weinrich, 1968; Westfall, 1995), as predicted by the Discourse Hypothesis (Hopper, 1979). Recall that background information is not temporally anchored (i.e., does not express events in chronological order) and it usually presents descriptions and commentaries. Although there are substantial studies that confirm that the imperfect is commonly used to express background information, other investigations have stated that the imperfect can also be used to express foreground information (Delgado-Díaz, 2014, 2018b; Gonzales, 1995; Gutiérrez-Araus, 1998; Reyes, 1990).

Theoretical investigations have attributed different hypotheses to explain the imperfect expressing foreground information. For example, Gutiérrez-Araus (1998) argued that the imperfect in foreground contexts, as illustrated in (3.22), is limited to literary works and is seldom used in spoken narrative. On the contrary, Gonzales (1995) mentioned that the imperfect can express foreground information (p.81) when recounting past habitual events. Consequently, this scholar argued that *llamaba* 'he would call', *venía* 'he would come', and *regaba* 'he would pour' in (3.23) all express foreground information since they depict the main events of the narration. Finally, Reyes (1990) stated that rupture imperfect can be found at the end of a series of events that are expressed by the preterit. This implies that this use of the imperfect expresses foreground information, as illustrated in (3.24). This scholar stated that *establecía* 'stablished' is stylistic and it is meant to hold the events, as if a portrait (Reyes, 1990: 55).

(3.22) En aquel momento preciso, solitario como había vivido, **moría** el famoso poeta. (Gutiérrez-Araus, 1998: 300)
In that precise moment, solitary as he had lived, died the famous poet.

(3.23) mi papá lo **llamaba** y él **venía**… y…echaba un poco de e- de un **regaba** un poco de agua en la tierra. (Gonzales, 1995: 79)
my father would call him and he would come…and…he would pour a little- of a [sic] would sprinkle a little water on the ground. (Translation taken from Gonzales, 1995: 79–80)

(3.24) AI amanecer salió el regimiento, atravesó Ia montaña, y poco después *establecía* contacto con el enemigo. (Reyes, 1990: 55)
At sunrise the cavalry exited, it passed the mountain, and after a short while established contact with the enemy.

Delgado-Díaz (2014, 2018b) also analyzed the preterit and imperfect with a variationist approach. Delgado-Díaz (2018b) found that the imperfect was favored by background information in Buenos Aires Spanish. However, there were ten cases (22.2%) of the imperfect expressing foreground information. On the contrary, type of discourse was not significant in Puerto Rican Spanish (Delgado-Díaz, 2014, 2018b). These findings imply that the imperfect can be used in limited contexts to express foreground information. Additionally, type of information does not function similarly cross-dialectally. Consequently, the imperfect is susceptible to language variation and change, which presents a fruitful area of diachronic research.

3.3.4 Review of the imperfect

This section reviewed studies that analyzed the aspectual functions, lexical semantic restrictions, and discourse functions of the imperfect. Regarding its aspectual function, various studies argue that the imperfect is typically used to express habitual or progressive events (Baker & Quesda, 2011; Bello, 1847; Bybee et al., 1994; Cipria & Roberts, 2000; Comrie, 1976; Delgado-Díaz, in press; Lamanna, 2008, 2012; Montrul & Slabakova, 2003; RAE, 1973, 2010; Rodríguez-Ramalle, 2005). However, there is substantial evidence of the imperfect expressing a perfective function (Ayres, 2009; Baker & Quesada, 2011; Delgado-Díaz, in press; Doiz, 2011; Rodriguez, 2004; Silva-Corvalán, 1994; Zentella, 1997). Ayres (2009), Silva-Corvalán (1994), and Zentella (1997) argued that this phenomenon is an effect of contact with English. However, this phenomenon has been documented in non-contact Spanish (Ayres, 2009; Baker & Quesada, 2011; Doiz, 2011; Rodríguez, 2004). Recall that, even though Ayres (2009) concluded that the imperfect with a perfective function is contact induced, this scholar found uses of the imperfect with this aspectual function in non-contact Spanish. Finally, Delgado-Díaz (in press) found that the imperfect main functions are progressiveness and habituality, but it can be used in limited cases to express a perfective aspectual function.

The second part of this section reviews previous studies on the imperfect regarding its lexical semantic restrictions. Various investigations state that the imperfect is associated with state and activity verbs (Acero, 1990; Alcina Franch & Blecua, 1975; Bardovi-Harlig, 2000;

Cipria & Roberts, 2000; Delgado-Díaz, 2014, 2018b; Montrul, 2002; Montrul & Slabakova, 2003; RAE, 1973, 2010; Rojas, 2015; Westfall, 1995). However, there is evidence of the imperfect with accomplishment and achievement verbs (Cipria & Roberts, 2000; Delgado-Díaz, 2014, 2018b; Rojas, 2015; Westfall, 1995). Delgado-Díaz (2014, 2018b) found that the imperfect is used more frequently with state and activity verbs, and less frequently with accomplishment and achievement verbs. Additionally, these quantitative analyses have discovered cross-dialect differences regarding the imperfect's lexical semantic restrictions. For instance, Delgado-Díaz (2014, 2018b) found that accomplishment verbs favor the imperfect in Puerto Rican Spanish. Additionally, Rojas (2015) found that stative verbs did not favor the use of the imperfect in Mexican Spanish. These findings suggest that the imperfect is not categorically used with state and activity verbs, rather, it is more probable to appear with these verbs (Bardovi-Harlig, 2000). Additionally, Delgado-Díaz' (2014, 2018b) and Rojas' (2015) results indicate that lexical semantic restrictions are susceptible to language variation and change.

The last part of this section revises previous studies on the discourse functions that the imperfect can convey. Most investigations mention that the imperfect is mainly used to express background information (Delgado-Díaz, 2018b; Gutiérrez-Araus, 1998; Silva-Corvalán, 1983; Soto, 2011; Westfall, 1995). However, there is evidence that the imperfect can be used with foreground information (Delgado-Díaz, 2018b; Gonzales, 1995; Gutiérrez-Araus, 1998; Reyes, 1990). Additionally, Delgado-Díaz (2018b) found that discourse function was significant in Buenos Aires Spanish, but it was not selected in Puerto Rican Spanish.

This review suggests that the imperfect is a complex aspectual form which is susceptible to variation and language change. Even though previous investigation describes the imperfect as stable and non-variable, quantitative data have found that the factors that predict its use vary cross-dialectally. Additionally, these studies document that the predictions of the Discourse Hypothesis (Hopper, 1979) and the Lexical Aspect Hypothesis (Andersen & Shirai, 1996) are probabilistic, as proposed by Bardovi-Harlig (2000). Consequently, the imperfect is a productive venue of diachronic research.

3.4 Present perfect

3.4.1 Aspectual functions

The present perfect is commonly interpreted as an anterior or perfect which signals a past event that has relevance in the present (Bybee et al., 1994; Comrie, 1976). However, according to Grammaticalization

Theory, perfect grams can develop into perfectives (Bybee et al., 1994). This topic has been the focus of many investigations which study the perfect-to-perfective grammaticalization of the Spanish present perfect (Burgo, 2010; Copple, 2011; Delgado-Díaz & Ortiz-López, 2011; Dumont, 2013; García-Negroni, 1999; Hernández, 2004, 2008; Holmes & Balukas, 2011; Howe & Schwenter, 2008; Jara-Yupanqui & Valenzuela Bismarck, 2013; Montero Cádiz, 2015; Ocampo, 2008; Rodríguez-Louro, 2009, 2010; Rodríguez-Louro & Howe, 2010; Rodríguez-Louro & Jara-Yupanqui, 2011; Schwenter, 1994; Schwenter & Torres Cacoullos, 2008; Serrano, 1996, among other) (see Howe, 2013 for an overview). Some investigations have found evidence that support the grammaticalization of the present perfect to perfective contexts (Burgo, 2010; Copple, 2011; Hernández, 2004, 2008; Holmes & Balukas, 2011; Howe, 2006; Howe & Schwenter, 2008; Jara-Yupanqui & Valenzuela Bismarck, 2013; Rodríguez-Louro & Jara-Yupanqui, 2011; Schwenter, 1994; Schwenter & Torres Cacoullos, 2008; Serrano, 1996). Several studies have found that this process occurs through indeterminate and hodiernal (i.e., events that occur within the same day) temporal references (Burgo, 2010; Copple, 2011; Hernández, 2004; Howe, 2006; Howe & Schwenter, 2008; Schwenter, 1994; Schwenter & Torres Cacoullos, 2008). For instance, Copple (2011) realized a diachronic investigation regarding the present perfect and preterit in Peninsular Spanish. The main objective of this investigation was to study the change of linguistic constraints that favor the use of the present perfect across centuries. Consequently, this investigation considered three periods: Old Spanish (15th century), Golden Age Spanish (17th century), and Modern Spanish (19th century).

Copple (2011) extracted 638 tokens from the 15th century (319 present perfect and 324 preterit), 1,546 items from the 17th century (775 present perfect and 771 preterit), and 1,502 cases from the 19th century (733 present perfect and 769 preterit). These tokens were coded for temporal reference (very recent, hodiernal, hesternal, pre-hesternal, irrelevant, and indeterminate), subject expression (pronominal, non-expressed, and lexical), lexical semantics (atelic, accomplishment, and achievement), and sentence mode (non-interrogative and interrogative). The statistical analysis was performed using GoldVarb X.

Table 3.1, taken from Copple (2011: 177), illustrates the results of the statistical analysis. According to this table, the present perfect experienced changes in linguistic constraints throughout the centuries. For instance, indeterminate and hodiernal temporal frame of reference disfavored the present perfect in the 15th century. However, indeterminate contexts favor this form in the 17th and 19th centuries while hodiernal contexts favor it in the 19th century. On the contrary, sentence

Table 3.1 Results of the statistical analysis according to the time period (Copple, 2011: 177)

Factor	15th century	17th century	19th century
Temporal reference			
Very recent	.61	.74	.75
Irrelevant	.54	.83	.83
Indeterminate	.47	.61	.64
Hodiernal	.2	.42	.54
Pre-hodiernal	[0]	.02	.09
Range	41	81	74
Subject expression			
Pronominal	.67	.62	.57
Expressed	.52	.47	.47
Lexical	.41	.52	.56
Range	26	15	10
Lexical semantics			
Atelic	.58	[.53]	.54
Accomplishment	.45	[.50]	.50
Achievement	.38	[.45]	.44
Range	20		10
Sentence mode			
Non-interrogative	.51	[.51]	[.49]
Interrogative	.47	[.46]	[.58]
Range	4		

Non-significant groups are shown in brackets

mode experienced the opposite effect. This factor was significant in the 15th century, but it did not reach significance in the 17th and 19th centuries. Copple (2011) highlights the fact that very recent temporal reference favors the use of the present perfect in the three time periods analyzed. This scholar argues that the present perfect with a resultative function (a present event that is the result of a past action) had already been generalized to the very recent past in the 15th century. Subsequently, the present perfect extended to irrelevant and indeterminate contexts in the 17th century. Lastly, the present perfect extended to hodiernal contexts in the 19th century.

Furthermore, Copple (2011) stated that the continued emergence of the present perfect in perfective context is represented by the increased favoring effect of indeterminate and hodiernal temporal references (p.177). However, it is important to keep in mind that the analysis included variable and non-variable contexts of the present perfect. Consequently, it is possible that these results do not reflect that extension of the present perfect to perfective contexts. This issue is discussed at the end of this section.

On the contrary, there are several studies that have found evidence that the present perfect is not grammaticalizing to perfective contexts (Dumont, 2013; Delgado-Díaz, in press; Delgado-Díaz & Ortiz-López, 2011; Henderson, 2010; Ocampo, 2008; Rodríguez-Louro, 2009, 2010). These investigations have found that temporal proximity and indetermination do not affect the use of the present perfect (Dumont, 2013; Delgado-Díaz & Ortiz-López, 2011; Rodríguez-Louro, 2009, 2010) and it has an overall low frequency of use (Delgado-Díaz, in press; Delgado-Díaz & Ortiz-López. 2011; Henderson, 2010; Rodríguez-Louro, 2009, 2010). For example, Rodríguez-Louro (2010) argued that the perfect-to-perfective grammaticalization of the present perfect caused by its perfective use in hodiernal contexts does not occur in Argentinean Spanish (p.16). This scholar investigated the use of the preterit and present perfect in this dialect. The participants were 30 speakers (13 men and 17 women) in the casual conversation, and 38 speakers (19 men and 19 women) in the sociolinguistic interview. The study found a total of 162 items (10%) of the present perfect and 1,397 tokens (90%) of the preterit. The present perfect was used 55% of the time to express an experimental function (i.e., past events that have been experienced at least once before and lead up to the present).

Rodríguez-Louro (2010) did not find evidence of the present perfect grammaticalizing to perfective contexts because it is not used in hodiernal temporal contexts. On the contrary, this scholar found that the present perfect is losing ground to preterit. The preterit is used to express a perfective function in hodiernal contexts, as illustrated in (3.25). Consequently, this could mean that the perfect-to-perfective grammaticalization does not operate in all Spanish dialects. On the contrary, Rodríguez-Louro's research suggests that the preterit could grammaticalize to perfect contexts.

(3.25) Hoy me *levanté* tipo 10 de la mañana. (Rodríguez-Louro, 2010: 18)
Today I got up at 10 in the morning. (Translation taken from Rodríguez-Louro, 2010: 18)

Similar results were found by Delgado-Díaz (in press). This scholar investigated the use of past forms in Puerto Rican Spanish to identify variable contexts with perfective, progressive, and habitual aspectual functions. This study coded for a total of 4,680 past expressions, which included the imperfect, the preterit, the imperfect progressive with *estar*, the preterit progressive with *estar*, the present perfect, and the simple present. Regarding the present perfect, Delgado-Díaz (in press) found five cases (.1%) of the present perfect with a perfective function, as illustrated in (3.26). Delgado-Díaz (in press) argued that the present perfect is not grammaticalizing to perfective in contexts in Puerto Rican Spanish.

(3.26) ...papi, se **ha parado** papi de aquel sillón, lo que papi decía casi temblando...
...dad, dad has gotten up form that armchair, he said almost trembling... (Delgado-Díaz, in press: 16)

It is worth mentioning that most variationist studies on the present perfect, except for Delgado-Díaz (in press), include all cases of this in the analysis and contrast it with the preterit. This may be problematic for two reasons: first, the analysis included variable contexts (perfective uses of the present perfect) and non-variable contexts (perfect uses of the present perfect). Consequently, these studies are not functional and present the factors that predict the use of the present perfect in general. This type of methodology may not necessarily illustrate the factors that predict the use of the present perfect with a perfective function. Delgado-Díaz (2018a) argues that researchers must identify the aspectual function of the present perfect and include in the analysis those cases that express a perfective function. This functional approach should determine the factors that predict the use of the present perfect with a perfective function.

The second problem that faces this methodology is that it assumes that only the preterit and present perfect vary within the perfective domain. However, other forms, such as the simple present, can express perfectivity. There is substantial evidence of the simple present expressing past perfective events (Bonilla, 2011; Delgado-Díaz, in press; Mayberry, 2011; Silva-Corvalán, 1984; Van Ess-Dykema, 1984). This implies that variation withing the perfective domain involves forms outside the present perfect–preterit paradigm. This issue is discussed elsewhere because it falls outside the scope of the present study.

3.4.2 Lexical semantics

This section reviews the lexical semantics attributed to the present perfect. The revision focuses on Grammaticalization Theory because it predicts that lexical semantic restrictions are weakened or lost as the present perfect grammaticalizes to perfective contexts (Schwenter &

Torres Cacoullos, 2008). This means that as this form grammaticalizes to perfective contexts, its lexical semantic restrictions weaken. This effect was documented by Copple (2011), who found that the present perfect was favored by atelic verbs in Old Spanish (p=.58) and Modern Spanish (p=.54). However, this factor did not reach statistical significance in Golden Age Spanish. Copple (2011) explained that even though this factor was significant in Modern Spanish, the lexical semantic effect is quite weak. Furthermore, this scholar interprets these results as the present perfect loses its aspectual value and gains a temporal status.

On the contrary, there are dialects in which the weakening of the present perfect lexical semantic restrictions has not been documented. This line of investigation argues that this construction does not have a high degree of grammaticalization or is not grammaticalizing (Burgo, 2010; Dumont, 2013; Delgado-Díaz & Ortiz-López, 2011; Hernández, 2004; Rodríguez-Louro, 2009; Schwenter & Torres Cacoullos, 2008[4]). In fact, Rodríguez-Louro (2009) found that the present perfect gained lexical semantic restriction in the diachronic axis. This scholar analyzed Argentinian written data from three time periods (period I 1810–1898, period II 1910–1970, and period III 1982–2007). The analysis revealed that lexical semantics was not significant in periods I and II, but it reached statistical significance in period III, in which the present perfect was favored by atelic verbs (p=.77). Rodríguez-Louro (2009) stated that this finding is due to the high frequency of the present perfect in continuative contexts. This result resonates with other studies that have found that the present perfect is favored by atelic verbs in cases in which it is not highly grammaticalized (Burgo, 2010; Dumont, 2013; Delgado-Díaz & Ortiz-López, 2011; Hernández, 2004; Schwenter & Torres Cacoullos, 2008).

3.4.3 Discourse function

This section reviews the discursive functions attributed to the present perfect. More specifically, this section focuses on previous investigations dealing with the type of information (i.e., foreground and background) that the present perfect can express. The debate regarding the present perfect and the type of information pertains to whether it can express foreground information since this role is traditionally expressed by perfective forms (Bybee et al., 1994: 62; Hopper, 1979: 215). Consequently, several studies have considered the discourse function of the present perfect in light of the perfect-to-perfective grammaticalization path (Hernández, 2004; Jara-Yupanqui, 2017; Jara-Yupanqui & Valenzuela Bismarck, 2013; Rodríguez-Louro & Howe, 2010). Their main premise is that the present perfect can express foreground information in dialects in which it is highly grammaticalized to perfective contexts because this discourse function is associated with the preterit (Jara-Yupanqui & Valenzuela Bismarck, 2013; Rodríguez-Louro & Howe, 2010).

Jara-Yupanqui and Valenzuela Bismarck (2013) and Rodríguez-Louro and Howe (2010) found evidence that the present perfect can express foreground information in Peruvian-Amazonian Spanish (as illustrated in (3.27); Jara-Yupanqui & Valenzuela Bismarck, 2013) and with hodiernal temporal references in Peninsular Spanish (as illustrated in (3.28); Rodríguez-Louro & Howe, 2010). However, Jara-Yupanqui and Valenzuela Bismarck (2013) and Rodríguez-Louro and Howe (2010) did not present the distribution of the present perfect with foreground information, which makes it difficult to determine its frequency of use.

(3.27) Veo bastante mamey arriba. Voy a subir a ese mamey a cogé. *He subido* arriba. Y había un mamey en la punta que era asizazo. Yo le quería coger ese de allí. Total la rama se *ha quebrado*. Yo me *he quedado* colgada pues allí.... (Jara-Yupanqui & Valezuela Bismarck, 2013: 49)
I see enough mamey [a type of fruit] up there. I'm going to climb that mamey tree to get some. I have gotten up. And there was a mamey in tip that was asizazo[5]. I wanted to take that one from there. The branch has broken. I have stayed hanging there...

(3.28) Me *he levantado* a las nueve de la mañana. *He desayunado* en casa. Me *[he] hecho* la comida. *He ido* a la casa de mis padres para hacer unas burocracias, y luego *he venido* a la universidad. (Rodríguez-Louro & Howe, 2010: 163)
I got up at...at 9 o'clock in the morning. I ate breakfast at home. (I) made lunch. I went to my parents' house to take care of some business, and then I came to the university.
(Translation taken from Rodríguez-Louro & Howe, 2010: 163)

Other studies have found that the present perfect is not highly grammaticalized to perfective contexts. Consequently, it is not frequently used to express foreground information (Hernández, 2004; Jara-Yupanqui, 2017). For instance, Jara-Yupanqui (2017) investigated the present perfect in Lima Spanish with the goal of investigating how this form is used in narratives. This scholar coded for chronological order, among other variables. The results indicate that the present perfect was not favored by chronological order, which could imply that this form is not used frequently to express foreground information.

3.4.4 Summary of the present perfect

This section reviews various investigations that studied the aspectual function of the present perfect. This form has been widely studied because of the perfect-to-perfective grammaticalization process. Consequently, the present perfect can express a perfective aspectual function, which has been documented in several studies. However, there is evidence that suggests that this process does not operate in all Spanish dialects. In fact, it is possible for the preterit to move to semantic areas of the present perfect (Delgado-Díaz, 2018a; Rodríguez-Louro, 2009, 2010). Therefore, the present perfect may present dialectal variation regarding its degree of grammaticalization within the perfect-to-perfective grammaticalization cline (Howe, 2006; Howe & Schwenter, 2008; Schwenter, 1994; Schwenter & Torres Cacoullos, 2008). Additionally, the present perfect can demonstrate dialectal variation with respect to its degree of entrenchment as it loses ground to the preterit (Rodríguez-Louro, 2010).

This survey also reviewed some investigations regarding the lexical semantic constraints attributed to the present perfect. These studies were guided by the Grammaticalization Theory since it predicts that lexical semantic constraints are weakened and eventually lost as the present perfect grammaticalizes as a perfective marker (Schwenter & Torres Cacoullos, 2008). Copple's (2011) research documented this process in Peninsular Spanish. On the contrary, Rodríguez-Louro (2009) showed that the present perfect can acquire lexical semantic restrictions when it loses ground to the preterit.

Finally, this survey suggests that the present perfect, once it develops a perfective function, can express foreground information. This tendency was found in Peninsular Spanish (Rodríguez-Louro & Howe, 2010) and in Peruvian-Amazonian Spanish (Jara-Yupanqui & Valenzuela Bismarck, 2013). However, Rodríguez-Louro and Howe (2010) suggest that the present perfect may develop other discourse functions, such as subjectivity, temporal indeterminacy, and evidentiality (Escobar, 1997). Consequently, Rodríguez-Louro and Howe (2010) suggest that the present perfect may develop differently cross-dialectally.

This summary of the present perfect demonstrates that further research is required with respect to its grammaticalization process. An issue that needs to be addressed pertains to the inclusion criteria of the present perfect. Recall that variationist investigation analyzes every use of the present perfect, which includes variable and non-variable contexts. This methodology does not present a clear picture of the development of this construction as a perfective marker. Consequently, the present perfect needs to be studied under a functional methodology to determine the factors that predict its use with a perfective aspectual function (Delgado-Díaz, 2018a).

3.5 Imperfect progressive

3.5.1 Aspectual function

This section examines previous investigations regarding the aspectual functions attributed to the imperfect progressive. This construction is commonly associated with a progressive aspectual function (King & Suñer, 1980; López-Otero & Cuza, 2020; Quesada, 1993; Solé & Solé, 1976; Westfall, 1995). More precisely, this construction expresses overt and unfolding events (King & Suñer 1980). Consequently, this has led researchers to state that the imperfect progressive cannot express habituality (Westfall, 1995). In fact, Westfall (1995) stated that sentences with an imperfect progressive expressing habitual events, as the one in (3.29), are ungrammatical.

(3.29) *Juan estaba escuchando música todos los días. (Westfall, 1995: 321)
John was listening to music every day. (Translation taken from Westfall, 1995: 321)

However, there is evidence that the imperfect progressive can be used in habitual contexts (Delgado-Díaz, in press; Delgado-Díaz & Galarza, 2019; Lamanna, 2008, 2012). Some of these studies claim that the extension of the imperfect progressive to habitual contexts is due to language contact with English (Lamanna, 2008). On the contrary, Lamanna (2012) and Delgado-Díaz and Galarza (2019) argue that this extension is not due to contact with English. Delgado-Díaz and Galarza (2019) investigated the use of the imperfect progressive in Puerto Rican Spanish. This research included Spanish–English bilinguals and Spanish monolinguals. The results indicate that knowledge of English did not predict the use of the imperfect progressive. Additionally, this construction was used 203 times (2.9%) of which eight cases were used in habitual contexts, as illustrated in (3.30). These scholars argue that the imperfect progressive in Puerto Rican Spanish is slowly grammaticalizing as an imperfective marker, as predicted by Grammaticalization Theory (Bybee et al., 1994).

(3.30) …yo me acuerdo de pai era que todos los domingos ***estaba*** presente ***viendo*** las carreras del hipódromo aquí en la tele… (Delgado-Díaz, in press)
…I remember that every Sunday dad was here watching horse races here in the t.v… (Translation taken from Delgado-Díaz, in press)

3.5.2 Lexical semantic

This section examines the lexical semantics attributed to the imperfect progressive. Most theoretical investigations argue that the imperfect progressive can only be used with dynamic verbs (i.e., activity and accomplishment verbs) (Quesada, 1993; Westfall, 1995). In fact, Westfall (1995) claims that the imperfect progressive is usually not acceptable with stative or accomplishment verbs. This scholar added that if the imperfect progressive is used with these verb classes, it has different interpretations. For example, it is interpreted as an event with stative verbs (p.322). This means that *tener* 'to have' in (3.31) is not interpreted as a state but rather as an event, although Westfall (1995) does not clearly explain what exactly is meant by event. When this construction is used with achievement verbs, it focuses on the preliminary stages of the event. This means that the subject in (3.32) had not died. However, these interpretations may be problematic because Westfall (1995) states that these uses entail different interpretations, contrary to Poplack's (2018) arguments in favor of syntactic neutralization.

(3.31) Elena ***estaba teniendo*** problemas con sus padres. (Westfall, 1995: 322)
Elena was having problems with her parents (Translation taken from Westfall, 1995: 322)

(3.32) Supe que se ***estaba muriendo***. (Westfall, 1995: 314)
I found out that he was dying. (Translation taken from Westfall, 1995: 314)

Quantitative studies have found that the imperfect progressive can be used with other verb classes (Delgado-Díaz & Galarza, 2019; Ramos-Pellicia, 1999). Ramos-Pellicia (1999) claimed that the use of this construction with achievement verbs is due to contact with English. This scholar investigated the factors that predict the use of the imperfect progressive with accomplishment and achievement verbs in Puerto Rican Spanish. The imperfect progressive with telic verbs was favored

Previous studies on Spanish past forms 49

by participants that were educated in Puerto Rico as opposed to those with education in the U.S. Additionally, the progressive with telic verbs was favored by students who spoke English and Spanish outside of their house. Ramos-Pellicia (1999) argues that the fact that speakers with less education in English used more progressive with telic verbs is due to the imperfect acquisition of English. She explains, following Thomason and Kaufman (1988), that imperfect acquisition of English may cause interference at the syntax, phonetic, and morphology levels. However, this conclusion is problematic because Ramos-Pellicia (1999) did not assess participants' level of English. Additionally, this hypothesis does not consider that grammaticalizing constructions expand their contexts of use after losing semantic restrictions.

More recently, Delgado-Díaz and Galarza (2019) found that the imperfect progressive can be used with all verb classes (states, activities, accomplishments, achievements, cognitive, and perceptual). However, they noted that this construction is primarily used with activity (33%) and accomplishment (38.9%) verbs, while it is scarcely used with state (3.9%), achievement (13.3%), cognitive (3.4%), and perception (6.9%) verbs. These scholars suggest that the imperfect progressive is gradually grammaticalizing as an imperfective marker, which implies that it extends to other semantic classes.

3.5.3 Discourse function

This section examines the discourse functions attributed to the imperfect progressive; more specifically, this section discusses investigations that analyze the type of information that this form can convey. The scarce studies on this topic argue that the imperfect progressive expresses background information (Gonzales, 1995; Mrak, 1998; Silva-Corvalán, 1983). Gonzales (1995) stated that the imperfect progressive is used to frame the events of the narrative. Consequently, *estaba jugando* 'I was playing' in (3.33) situates the event in which the top flew. Similarly, Mrak (1998) found that the imperfect progressive can be used to express background information in Houston Spanish. However, it is difficult to determine its frequency of use with background information because Gonzales (1995) conducted a theoretical research and Mrak (1998) does not present its distribution with background information

(3.33)   Casualmente tengo aquí en la frente un recuerdo de que *estaba jugando* con otro niño y él... fue- enredó el trompo el- la cuerda pero no la no la enredó bien y cuando lo fue a tirar estaba floja y el trompo salió. (Gonzales, 1995: 72)

Incidentally, I have here on my forehead a souvenir from when I was playing with another child and he...was- he wound the top the the cord but didn't didn't wind it well and when he went to throw it it was loose and the top flew. (Translation taken from Gonzales, 1995: 72)

Silva-Corvalán (1983) presents an insight into the frequency of use of the imperfect progressive expressing background information. Recall that this scholar investigated the distribution of tense and aspect in 27 Chilean and three Mexican narratives. The results regarding the imperfect progressive show that there were ten cases (7%) of this construction expressing background information. These results suggest that the imperfect progressive is not used frequently to express background information.

3.5.4 Summary of the imperfect progressive

This section examines previous research regarding the aspectual functions, lexical semantics, and discourse functions attributed to the imperfect progressive. Regarding aspectual function, this construction is mainly associated with a progressive function (Delgado-Díaz, in press; Delgado-Díaz & Galarza, 2019; King & Suñer, 1980; López-Otero & Cuza, 2020; Quesada, 1993; Solé & Solé, 1976; Westfall, 1995). Additionally, there is evidence that indicates that it can also express a habitual aspectual function (Delgado-Díaz, in press; Delgado-Díaz & Galarza, 2019; Lamanna, 2008, 2012). However, Delgado-Díaz (in press) and Delgado-Díaz and Galarza (2019) found that it is used in limited cases to express a habitual function in Puerto Rican Spanish.

With respect to the lexical semantics attributed to this construction, various investigations argue that it is used with dynamic and durative verbs (i.e., activities and accomplishments). On the contrary, there is evidence that indicates that the imperfect progressive can be used with other verb classes as well (Delgado-Díaz & Galarza, 2019; King & Suñer, 1980; Ramos-Pellicia, 1999). Delgado-Díaz and Galarza (2019) found that the imperfect progressive is mainly used with activity and accomplishment verbs and with less frequently with state, achievement, cognitive, and perception verbs. These results may suggest that this construction is grammaticalizing as a general imperfective (Bybee et al., 1994).

Regarding the discourse function of the imperfect progressive, there are few studies that have considered this factor, which argues that the imperfect progressive expresses background information (Gonzales,

1995; Mrak, 1998; Silva-Corvalán, 1983). However, Silva-Corvalán's (1983) research suggests that it is not used frequently to express background information.

It is worth highlighting that much of the debate regarding this construction focuses on language contact with English (Ayres, 2009; Chaston, 1991; Delgado-Díaz, 2018a; Delgado-Díaz & Galarza, 2019; Koontz-Garboden, 1999; Lamanna, 2008, 2012; López-Otero & Cuza, 2020; Mrak, 1998; Pousada & Poplack, 1979; Ramos-Pellicia, 1999). This line of research argues that increased frequency of use and the extension to habitual contexts and telic verbs is due to contact with English (Ayres, 2009; Koontz-Garboden, 1999; Lamanna, 2008; López-Otero & Cuza, 2020; Ramos-Pellicia, 1999). However, these effects are also predicted by Grammaticalization Theory. This theory states that grammaticalizing grams experience generalization, which refers to an extension to other contexts of use and an increase in frequency of use (Bybee, 2003a; Heine, 2003). Consequently, this implies that the patterns of variation of the imperfect progressive may reflect a grammaticalization process rather than English influence (Delgado-Díaz & Galarza, 2019). Recall that progressive constructions tend to grammaticalize as imperfect markers (Bybee et al., 1994). This issue is discussed elsewhere because it falls outside the scope of this book (Delgado-Díaz, in press). Nonetheless, this review suggests that the imperfect progressive is experiencing language change. Additionally, its discourse function has not been extensively studied. Consequently, a diachronic analysis may shed light on the development of this construction.

3.6 Preterit progressive

3.6.1 Aspectual function

The preterit progressive is associated with a dual perfective and progressive function (Comrie, 1976; Solé & Solé, 1976; Westfall, 1995, 2003). Solé and Solé (1976) described the preterit progressive as a terminated ongoing action in the past (p.50). According to these scholars, the use of the preterit progressive is used to highlight the ongoing aspect of a terminated event. Comrie (1976) made a similar distinction arguing that the use of the preterit progressive views the event as "a single complete whole" (p.23). This implies that the sentence in (3.34) includes the whole phases of the event. Similarly, Westfall (2003) stated that the preterit progressive entails a perfective progressive function. These descriptions may be problematic because these researchers want to create a contrast between the imperfect progressive and preterit progressive. However, syntactic variation may entail contexts in which two or more forms express similar meanings (i.e., neutralize contexts) (Poplack, 2018).

(3.34) Toda la tarde *estuvieron entrando* visitas. (Comrie, 1976: 22)
All evening guests were arriving/had arrived. (Translation taken from Comrie, 1976: 22)

However, Delgado-Díaz (in press) did not find that the preterit progressive entails a dual progressive and perfective aspectual function. Recall that this scholar investigated the different past forms in Puerto Rican Spanish with a variationist approach. The results indicate that the preterit progressive is used infrequently, 28 cases (.6% of the data) and it is mainly used to express a progressive function, 21 cases (72.4%[6]). The example in (3.35a) illustrates a case of the preterit progressive with a progressive function since it is modified by *un tiempito* 'a little while'. Additionally, Delgado-Díaz (in press) found that this construction was used once to express a habitual function. This scholar argues that the preterit progressive in (3.35b) expresses a habitual event because it is modified by *todo el tiempo* 'all the time'. Consequently, this implies that the preterit progressive mainly expresses a progressive function, but it can also express a habitual function with a considerably lower frequency.

(3.35) a. Y ahí, pues, *estuve trabajando* con ellos un tiempito...
And there, well, I was working with them for a little while...
(Delgado-Díaz, in press)
b. ...siempre lo que poníamos cuando llegábamos, era Super Smash Bros. y eso era melee y todo el tiempo estuvimos ahí y todo el tiempo *estuvimos* ahí y *jugando*...
...what we used to always play was Super Smash Bros. and that was melee and we were there all the time and all the time we were there and playing... (Delgado-Díaz, in press)

3.6.2 Lexical semantic

This section reviews the investigations which address the lexical semantic restrictions of the preterit progressive. The few studies that consider this topic have stated that the preterit progressive can only appear with dynamic verbs (i.e., activities and accomplishments) (Westfall, 1995, 2003). Westfall (1995, 2003) argued that there are some restrictions of the preterit progressive with stative verbs. Therefore, the sentence in (3.36) should not be acceptable to Spanish native speakers because it is a static event and does not admit a change of state (Westfall, 2003:

878). However, Westfall (2003) noted that the preterit progressive accepts some stative verbs. This scholar stated that the event presented in (3.37) is not interpreted as a stative event. According to Westfall (2003), the preterit progressive with some stative events shifts to an activity interpretation because it "focuses on the dynamic unfolding of a verbal action" (p.878). Additionally, Westfall, (1995, 2003) mentioned that this construction can be used with some achievement verbs, which presents the event as bounded and iterative. Consequently, the event of landing, in (3.38), is viewed as a "series of closed events within a large time interval" (p.878). However, Westfall (1995, 2003) does not present a quantitative analysis which makes it difficult to determine the frequency of use of the preterit progressive with these verb classes. Additionally, these readings may include a form-function asymmetry assumption (Poplack, 2018).

(3.36) *Juan *estuvo sabiendo* la verdad. (Westfall, 2003: 878)
*Juan was knowing the truth. (Translation taken from Westfall, 2003: 878)

(3.37) Juan *estuvo viviendo* en Madrid antes de mudarse para Buenos Aires. (Westfall, 2003: 878)
Juan was living in Madrid before moving to Buenos Aires. (Translation taken from Westfall, 2003: 878)

(3.38) El avión *estuvo aterrizando* a la hora. (Westfall, 2003: 878)
The airplane was landing within the hour. (Translation taken from Westfall, 2003: 878)

3.6.3 Discourse function

This section discusses previous investigations regarding the discursive function of the preterit progressive. To our knowledge, there is one study that address this topic (Westfall, 1995). Westfall (1995) mentioned that the preterit progressive expresses foreground information because it updates the narratives by introducing events in chronological order. The example in (3.39) presents a series of events in chronological order, which moves the narrative forward. According to Westfall (1995), the preterit progressive *estuvo mirando* 'was watching' presents foreground information because it expresses the events in chronological order (i.e., it occurred after eating dinner and before studying). It is worth mentioning that Westfall (1995) does not provide a quantitative analysis making it difficult to determine the frequency of use of the preterit progressive with foreground information.

(3.39) Anoche, Juan llegó a casa a las 5, cenó, *estuvo mirando* la tele un rato, estudió, y se acostó a las 11. (Westfall, 1995: 341) Last night, John arrived home at 5:00, ate dinner, was watching television for a while, studied, and went to bed at 11:00. (Translation taken from Westfall, 1995: 342)

3.6.4 Summary of the preterit progressive

This section revises previous investigations on the preterit progressive which analyzed its aspectual function, lexical semantic restrictions, and its discourse function. Regarding its aspectual function, theoretical studies have argued that the preterit progressive expresses a dual progressive and perfective aspectual function (Comrie, 1976; Solé & Solé, 1976; Westfall, 1995, 2003). However, Delgado-Díaz (in press) did not find that this construction expresses both perfectiveness and progressiveness. This scholar found that it is mainly used to express a progressive function and less frequently to convey a habitual function in Puerto Rican Spanish. With respect to its lexical semantic restriction, Westfall (1995, 2003) stated that this form can be used with statives, activities, accomplishments, and achievements. However, the preterit progressive has some restrictions and changes in the interpretation of the event. Finally, Westfall (1995) stated that this construction is used to express foreground information. However, there are few quantitative investigations focusing on the preterit progressive, which makes it difficult to determine its frequency of use within its aspectual functions, lexical semantic restrictions, and discourse function. Additionally, most of these theoretical analyses assume form-function symmetry in which the preterit progressive always expresses these grammatical functions. Poplack (2018) argued that syntactic variation is full of asymmetries and neutralized contexts. Therefore, the preterit progressive requires further quantitative research to understand how it works. Finally, this construction presents a unique opportunity to study its emergence and diachronic development.

3.7 Summary of the previous investigations

This chapter presented an overview of studies on the Spanish past aspectual forms. The forms considered were the preterit, imperfect, present perfect, imperfect progressive, and preterit progressive. Each form

Previous studies on Spanish past forms 55

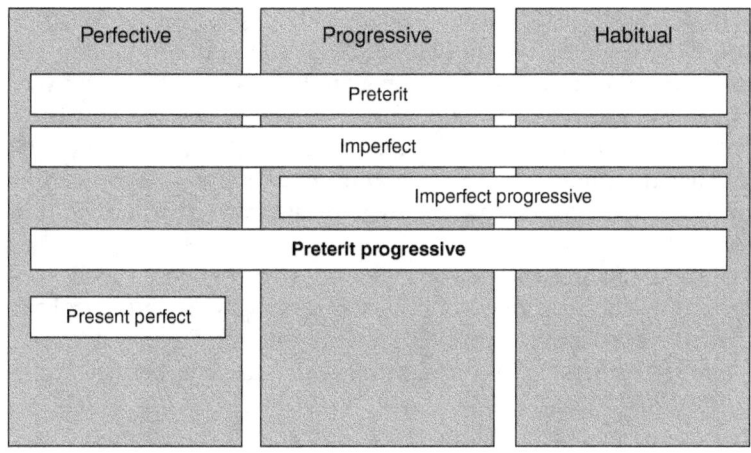

Figure 3.1 Representation of the aspectual functions according to the past form

was discussed based on the aspectual functions, lexical semantics, and discursive functions attributed to them. This section presents a summary of the most important aspects discussed throughout this chapter.

Regarding the aspectual function, this review found that the Spanish aspectual system is complex, and it exhibits many instances of form-function overlapping (Figure 3.1). Figure 3.1 is a visual representation of the different functions attributed to these forms, according to previous studies. This figure illustrates that the preterit, imperfect, and preterit progressive can convey perfective, habitual, and progressive functions. The imperfect progressive can express habitual and progressive events and the present perfect expresses perfective events.

Figure 3.1 also reveals that these forms have overlapping usage, which may suggest instances of layering (different forms competing over the same functional domain) and retention (a grammaticalizing gram retains older semantic nuances) (Bybee et al., 1994; Heine, 2003; Schwenter & Torres Cacoullos, 2008). Furthermore, this conceptual map may indicate that studying these forms in pairs (i.e., preterit vs imperfect, imperfect vs imperfect progressive) does not represent the complexity of the aspectual system since many forms can express the same function.

With respect to the lexical semantics, this chapter found that the preterit, imperfect, imperfect progressive, and preterit progressive can be used with all types of verbs (Acero, 1990; Alcina Franch & Blecua, 1975;

Cipria & Roberts, 2000; Delgado-Díaz, 2014, 2018b; King & Suñer, 1980; RAE, 1973, 2010; Ramos-Pellicia, 1999; Rojas, 2015; Westfall, 1995, 2003). However, Westfall (1995, 2003) stated that the interpretation of the events may shift depending on the aspectual form and verb type. For instance, when the imperfect is used with achievement verbs it focuses on the initial stages of the event. In addition, Westfall (1995) argued that the preterit progressive and imperfect progressive can be used with some stative verbs, but they are interpreted as events (i.e., activities).

Regarding the present perfect, this construction loses its lexical semantic restrictions in dialects in which it is highly grammaticalized as a perfective marker (Copple, 2011; Schwenter & Torres Cacoullos, 2008, among others). On the contrary, the present perfect seems to be constricted to activity and state verbs in dialects in which this construction is not highly grammaticalized or is losing ground to the preterit (Burgo, 2010; Dumont, 2013; Delgado-Díaz & Ortiz-López, 2011; Hernández, 2004; Rodríguez-Louro, 2009; Schwenter & Torres Cacoullos, 2008).

The last factor analyzed was the discursive function each form can convey. Several investigations argue that the imperfect and imperfect progressive are associated with background information (Delgado-Díaz, 2018b; Gonzales, 1995; Gutiérrez-Araus, 1998; Mrak, 1998; Silva-Corvalán, 1983; Soto, 2011; Reyes, 1990; Weinrich, 1968; Westfall, 1995). On the contrary, the preterit and preterit progressive are associated with foreground information (Bardovi-Harlig, 2000; Delgado-Díaz, 2018b; Silva-Corvalán, 1983; Weinrich, 1968; Westfall, 1995). However, Delgado-Díaz (2018b) found that, in limited cases, the imperfect can be used to express foreground information and the preterit can be used to express background information. Unfortunately, there are not sufficient empirical studies on the preterit progressive and imperfect progressive to determine their usage pattern with discourse function. The present perfect, once it develops a perfective function, can express foreground information (Jara-Yupanqui & Valenzuela Bismarck, 2013; Rodríguez-Louro & Howe, 2010). On the contrary, the present perfect expresses background information in dialect in which it is not highly grammaticalized (Hernández, 2004; Jara-Yupanqui, 2017).

It is worth mentioning some problems with previous investigations. First, several studies base their conclusion on theoretical analysis, which does not account for the frequency of use of these constructions. Second, while most investigations focus on the preterit, imperfect, and present perfect, there is a lack of empirical studies on the past progressive construction. Consequently, it is difficult to determine their distribution with respect to their aspectual function, lexical semantic restrictions, and discourse functions. Third, most investigations assume a form-function symmetry regarding the grammatical functions that these constructions can express. This implies that researchers attribute meanings to a construction when its function may be neutralized (Poplack, 2018). However, recent investigations argue that language is full of form-function asymmetries (Delgado-Díaz, in press; Poplack, 2018). Finally, variationist studies on the present perfect include variable and non-variable contexts in the analysis. This type of analysis becomes focus-on-form, rather than focus-on-function. Additionally, it was mentioned previously that the results of these investigations may not represent the factors that predict the use of the present perfect with a perfective function. Consequently, the issues presented here may imply that generalizations made regarding the aspectual functions (Figure 3.1), lexical semantic restrictions, and discourse functions of these constructions are not accurate. Therefore, further investigations are needed with a quantitative approach to present a clear picture of how these forms behave and how they interact with each other.

Notes

1 The reader is directed to Delgado-Díaz (2018a) for a detailed review.
2 It is not clear whether Ayres (2009) coded for the number of the subject or the object in this variable.
3 The exact usage of the preterit is unclear because Silva-Corvalán (1983) collapsed the preterit and preterit progressive.
4 The present perfect has lexical semantic restrictions in Mexican Spanish.
5 Could not find the meaning of this word. Could be an idiom from this particular dialect.
6 Delgado-Díaz coded six cases as indeterminate and one case as habitual.

4 The study

4.1 Rationale for the present study

The main goal of this investigation is to study the imperfect, preterit, imperfect progressive, preterit progressive, present perfect, and other past forms that can express habitual, progressive, and/or perfective functions in Spanish from a diachronic perspective. The motivation for this study stems from instances of language variation and change identified in the previous chapter. Consequently, this research allows us to track the emergence and development of Spanish past expressions. Additionally, including these forms would meet the requirements of the principle of accountability since an investigation needs to consider all forms that could serve similar functions (Poplack & Tagliamonte, 1999).

This investigation is guided by Gammaticalization Theory because it can explain diachronic changes (Poplack & Tagliamonte, 1999: 194) (see chapter 2). These changes can be observed by increased frequency and change of linguistic constrains (Bybee et al., 1994; Copple, 2011; Poplack & Tagliamonte, 1999; Torres Cacoullos, 2009, 2012). In Spanish, since the past progressive forms (i.e., preterit progressive, *estuve cantando*, and imperfect progressive, *estaba cantando*) were developed later than the morphological forms (Penny, 2000: 197), it is possible that the emergence of these forms has shifted the whole aspectual system. In fact, Grammaticalization Theory predicts that periphrastic forms usually replace morphological ones (Hopper & Traugott, 2003: 9), which may imply that the past progressive forms express similar functions as the morphological ones causing variable contexts.

Another issue that motivates this investigation is that previous investigations on tense and aspect in Spanish tend to examine past forms in a dichotomous fashion (i.e., preterit vs imperfect, imperfect vs imperfect progressive, preterit vs present perfect). This may be reflecting a definition of the object of study based on forms without taking into account the overlap of functions that some of these forms have, which does not account for the range of variation that may exist between Spanish past forms.

4.1.1 Research questions

The following research questions guide this investigation:

1. What are the patterns of variation found in the past-time expression in Spanish?
   What is the distribution of the imperfect, preterit, present perfect, imperfect progressive, and preterit progressive in Spanish diachronic data? Which forms have overlapping functions?
2. How does Grammaticalization Theory explain these patterns of variability?
   Do the linguistic factors that predict the use of different past forms change through time?

4.2 Methodology

These research questions aim at tracing the development of the past progressive forms in Spanish. The main purpose of this analysis is to identify the pattern of use of the different past-time expressions in Spanish. The next sections describe the methodology employed in this study.

4.2.1 The diachronic data

This study traces the uses of the Spanish past-time expression in Medieval Spanish (13th–15th century), Golden Age Spanish (17th century), and Modern Spanish (19th century), following Torres Cacoullos' (2009, 2012) methodology. The analysis focuses on novels that incorporate dialogs from Spanish authors. Table 4.1 shows the novels analyzed, the tokens extracted from each novel, the total token count in each period, and the approximate word count for each period. This analysis yielded a total of 5,286 past-time expressions. Additionally, two novels from each period were analyzed, following Torres Cacoullos' (2009, 2012) methodology on the present progressive.

The initial idea was to extract the first 1,000 tokens of past-time expressions from each novel, however, *El Cantar del Mio Cid* and *Los Locos de Valencia* were too short and did not allow to extract this quantity. Subsequentially, every past-time expression was extracted from these two literary works. Further items were extracted from *Caballero de Zifar*

60 The study

Table 4.1 Novels analyzed in the diachronic study (Torres Cacoullos, 2009, 2012)

Medieval Spanish	Golden Age	Modern Spanish
Caballero de Zifar 1,133 tokens El Cantar del Mio Cid 419 tokens Total 1,552 tokens Approx. 60,000 words	El Quijote 1,516 tokens Los Locos de Valencia 287 tokens Total 1,803 tokens Approx. 200,000 words	Pepita Jiménez 979 tokens Doña Perfecta 952 tokens Total 1,931 tokens Approx. 120,000 words

and *El Quijote* to reach representative token count. Furthermore, some tokens were discarded because the contexts were difficult to understand, such as *cojó* in *Martín Antolínez con ellos se cojó, vanse pora San Pero* (MC) 'Martín Antolínez "grouped up"? with them'. Additionally, cases such as *miró prometiéndomelo* in *por qué me miró prometiéndomelo todo* (PJ) 'why did he look at me promising me everything' were discarded from the analysis because they had a progressive like structure (i.e., verb + -construction) but are two separate units.

4.2.2 Coding scheme

This section exhibits the variables included in the analysis.
Dependent variable:

1. Past-time expression: this variable consists of the preterit (4.1a), preterit progressive (4.1b), imperfect (4.1c), imperfect progressive (4.1d), present perfect (4.1e), and other (preterit progressive with other auxiliary verbs, imperfect progressive with other auxiliary verbs) (4.1f).

It is worth highlighting some details regarding the present perfect. This construction was only included when it signaled a perfective event because perfect aspectual function falls outside the scope of this book. Several cues were considered when determining if a present perfect expressed a perfective function. First, the co-occurrence with *ya* 'already' was considered because this adverb can indicate that the event occurred before the utterance (Schwenter & Torres Cacoullos, 2008). In addition, it was considered if the event expressed with the present perfect was also expressed with the preterit. If the same event was expressed with both the preterit and the present perfect, it is likely that the present perfect signaled a perfective meaning. Additionally, the whole context

The study 61

was considered to determine if the event expressed by the present perfect was perfective. For example, in (4.1e) Erifila asked Floriano if he is married using the present perfect, which Floriano replies using the preterit. This indicates that the present perfect signaled a perfective event and, thus, it was included in the analysis.

Additionally, present forms were not included in the analysis because, even though they can express past events (RAE, 1973, 2010), it is difficult to determine if they have a past temporal reference in written discourse.

(4.1) a. E el fijo *se fue* e *levó* el saco e *ferió* a la puerta del medio amigo de su padre. E *salieron* a él los hombres y *preguntáronle* qué quería; e *díxoles* que quería fablar con el amigo de su padre, e ellos *fueron* gelo dezir, e *mandó* que entrase. (Caballero de Zifar)
And the son left and took the bag and knocked on his father's half friend's door. And the men came out and asked him what he wanted; and he told them that he wanted to speak with his father's friend, and they went to tell him that, and he ordered him to come in.

b. Toda esta larga arenga (que se pudiera muy bien excusar) dijo nuestro caballero, porque las bellotas que le dieron le trajeron a la memoria la edad dorada, y antojósele hacer aquel inútil razonamiento a los cabreros, que, sin respondelle palabra, embobados y suspensos le *estuvieron escuchando*. Sancho asimismo callaba, y comía bellotas y visitaba muy a menudo el segundo zaque, que porque se enfriase el vino lo tenían colgado de un alcornoque. (El Quijote)
All this long discourse (that could have been excused) said our knight, because the acorns that they gave him brought to memory the golden age, he fancied doing that futile reasoning to the knights, that, without answering him a word, dumbfounded and amazed were listening to him. Sancho at the same time was silent, and was eating acorns, and visited very frequently the second wineskin, that because it would get cold he had it hanging on a corn oak.

c. Pepita tendrá veinte años; es viuda; sólo tres años estuvo casada. *Era* hija de doña Francisca Gálvez, viuda, como usted sabe, de un capitán retirado, que le dejó a su muerte sólo su honrosa espada por herencia, según dice el poeta. (Pepita Jiménez)

Pepita would be twenty years old; she is a widow; she was married for only three years. She was the daughter of doña Francisaca Gálvez, widow, like you know, of a retired captain, that at his death he only left her his honorable sword as an inheritance, according to the poet.

d. —Yo estoy aquí muy bien—repuso Pepe—. Ahora le *estaba diciendo* a Rosario que esta ciudad y esta casa me son tan agradables, que me gustaría vivir y morir aquí. (Doña Perfecta)
—I am fine here—replied Pepe—. I was now telling Rosaria that this city and this house are so pleasant, that I would like to live and die here.

e. Erifila: Y dime, estás ya casado?
Floriano: Sí, Erifila, no ves al lado el alma de aqueste pecho?
Erifila: Que te *has casado*, traidor?
Floriano: Caséme, como te fuiste, y porque me aborreciste, teniendo á
Valerio amor. (Los Locos de Valencia)
Erifila: And tell me, are you married now?
Floriano: Yes, Erifila, don't you see the side the soul of this chest?
Erifila: You married, traitor?
Floriado: I married, because you left, and because you abhorred me, having Valerio's love.

f. Los demás *seguían guardando* silencio. (Doña Perfecta)
The others continue to remain in silence.

Independent variables:

1. Aspectual function: this variable includes habitual (an event that is repeated during an extensive period of time), progressive (an event as ongoing in the reference time), perfective (an event that has an end point and is completed) (Comrie, 1976; Bybee et al., 1994), and indeterminate. Aspectual function was included because previous investigations have attributed different aspectual functions to the same form (see Figure 3.1, chapter 3).

It is worth mentioning that a form-function symmetry was not assumed, following Poplack (2018). Aspectual function was coded according to contextual information provided by the adverbs and/or the discourse context. Furthermore, this investigation did not assume that alternate ways of expressing the same referential or grammatical meaning are a deviation of the norm (the form-function symmetry doctrine, Poplack & Dion, 2009; Poplack, 2018). In fact, form-function symmetry was rejected in light of Baker and Quesada's (2011) results, in which they found that Spanish native speakers could vary between different forms in contexts without adverbial contexts. For this reason, it is claimed that adverbs are crucial in terms of determining which aspectual function is intended by the speaker in his or her discourse. Consequently, the fragment in (4.2a) was coded as habitual because the adverb *cada día* indicated that it was a repeated event in the past. The item in (4.2b) was coded as progressive because *aún* 'still' indicates that the event was ongoing. The verb in (4.2c) was coded as perfective because *en seguida* 'immediately' indicated that the event happened once in the past. However, there were some cases in which there were no adverbs or discursive cues that indicated the aspectual function of the verb. For instance, *tuvieron* 'they had' and *fue* 'was' in (4.2d) were coded as indeterminate because the context does not allow us to determine if they are perfective or progressive.

(4.2) a. E otro día fueron fazer su oraçión a la eglesia e oyeron misa, que así lo *fazían* cada día ante que cavalgasen. (Caballero de Zifar)
And the next day they went to do their prayer at the church and they heard mass, as they did every day before riding.

b. …vinieron todos en gran deseo de saber más particularmente quién era, y aun de ayudarle si alguna fuerza le quisiesen hacer; y así, se fueron hacia la parte donde aún *estaba hablando* y porfiando con su criado. (El Quijote)
All came with great interest of knowing who he was, and to help him if they wanted to do any coercion, and like that, they went to where he still was talking and arguing with his servant.

c. En seguida me *asaltó* el pensamiento de que su amor mal pagado podría ser la causa de la enfermedad. (Pepita Jiménez)
Immediately the thought jumped me that her badly repaid love could be the cause of the sickness.

d. No ignoro que los varones religiosos y los santos, que deben servirnos de ejemplo y dechado, cuando *tuvieron* gran familiaridad y amor con mujeres *fue* en la ancianidad, o estando ya muy probados y quebrantados por la penitencia,

o existiendo una notable desproporción de edad entre ellos y las piadosas amigas que elegían; como se cuenta de San Jerónimo y Santa Paulina, y de San Juan de la Cruz y Santa Teresa. (Pepita Jiménez)
I don't ignore that religious males and saints, which should be our example and paragon, it was in old age when they had great familiarity and love with women or being very tested and broken already by penitence, or having a notable age difference between them and the compassionate friend they chose; like it is told of Saint Geronimo and Saint Paulina, and of Saint John of the Cross and Saint Teresa.

2. Lexical semantics: this variable includes Vendler's (1957) semantic classes, which are stative verbs, activity verbs, accomplishment verbs, and achievement verbs. According to Vendler (1957), state verbs are non-dynamic, atelic, and durative while activity verbs are dynamic, atelic, and durative. On the other hand, accomplishments are dynamic, telic, and durative, whereas achievement verbs are dynamic, telic, and punctual. In addition, this factor also includes cognitive and perception verbs (Aaron, 2006). Example (4.3a–f) shows samples of these different verb classes in the diachronic data. The fragment in (4.3a) illustrates a stative verb, (4.3b) an activity verb, (4.3c) an accomplishment verb, (4.3d) an achievement verb, (4.3e) a cognitive verb, and (4.3f) a perception verb.

(4.3) a. Hasta la edad de dieciséis años *vivió* Pepita con su madre en la mayor estrechez, casi en la miseria. (Pepita Jiménez)
Until the age of sixteen Pepita lived with her mother in great hardship, almost in misery.

b. Los vassallos de mio Cid sin piedad les *davan*, en un ora e un poco de logar trezientos moros matan. (El Cantar del Mio Cid)
The Mio Cid's vassals hit them without mercy, within a little more than an hour they manage to kill three hundred Muslims

c. ¿Dexas el alma y la vida, y formas agravio dellas? Si estas dos cosas te *dí*, quando á mis padres dexé ... (Los Locos de Valencia)
You leave your soul and life, and you make grievance of them? If I gave you these two things, when I left my parents ...

d. Y al instante *se alzó* también sobre los estribos para mirar. (Doña Perfecta)
And in an instant he also raised himself on the stirrups to look.

e. Adeliñar tras mio Cid, el bueno de Bivar, tres días e dos noches *pensaron* de andar. (El Cantar del Mio Cid)
Adeliñar and Mio Cid, the good man from Bivar, thought about riding for three days and two nights.

f. Todas estas pláticas *estaba escuchando* muy atento Don Quijote. (El Quijote)
Don Quijote was listening carefully to all these conversations.

Cognitive and perception verbs were incorporated in the analysis because of several criticisms to Vendler's semantic classes (Filip, 2011). Recall that Filip (2011) mentioned that one of the criticisms is the notion that some stative verbs can shift to an active semantic class. This may imply that cognitive and perception verbs may entail some dynamicity making them compatible with progressive constructions. Example (4.3f) illustrates a case of a perception verb *escuchar* 'to hear' in the imperfect progressive. On the contrary, stative verbs will tend to appear in the simple forms since they usually express non-dynamic events while achievement verbs will not tend to appear in the progressive forms because they are punctual. In addition, several predictions can be drawn from this fact. For instance, it is expected that states and activities will favor the imperfect while accomplishments and achievements will favor the preterit, following the Aspect Hypothesis (Andersen & Shirai, 1996). It is important to highlight the fact that the whole context (the verb and its arguments) was examined in order to classify the tokens because the semantic class of a verb can shift depending on its arguments used (Dowty, 1977, 1979; 1986; Salas-Gonzáles, 1996; Verkuyl, 1972, 2005, 2012; Westfall, 1995).

3. Type of information: this variable incorporated foreground and background information (Hopper, 1979; Silva-Corvalán, 1983; Westfall, 1995). Foreground information moves the narrative forward and reflects the chronological order of the events of a narrative. On the contrary, background information presents descriptions, commentaries, etc. that provided supporting details regarding the main events of the narrative and it does not move the narrative forward (Hopper, 1979). In order to have a systematic coding criteria for this factor, it was verified if the clause was introduced by a

conjunction because background information is usually introduced by a conjunction (*que* 'that', *porque* 'because', etc.). For example, the fragment in (4.4) mentions that Don Quijote had placed his weapons on top of a well. One mule driver moved them to give water to his mules. Subsequently, Don Quijote hit the mule driver on the head with his spear and placed his weapons on top of the well. Afterwards, another mule driver comes with the same intention as the previous one. In this fragment, (4.4a) was coded as background information since it is introduced by a conjunction (*porque* 'because') and it provides a description of what had happened. On the contrary, *llegó* in (4.4b) was coded as foreground information because it informs the reader of what happens next in the story (i.e., the chronological order of the events).

(4.4) Desde allí a poco, sin saberse lo que había pasado (porque aún ***estaba*** (a) aturdido el arriero), ***llegó*** (b) otro con la misma intención de dar agua a sus mulos. (El Quijote)
A little while later, without knowing what had happened (because the mule driver was still stunned), another arrived with the same intention of giving water to the mules.

However, not all cases of background information were introduced by a conjunction. In these cases, the whole context was examined to determine the type of information. For example, *producían* 'produced' in (4.5) was coded as background information because it provides a description of the sound that the train was making. The distinction between foreground and background clauses is important because foreground information tends to appear more with the preterit while the imperfect tends to appear with background information (Hopper, 1979).

(4.5) Antes de que la caravana se pusiese en movimiento, partió el tren, que se iba escurriendo por la vía con la parsimoniosa cachaza de un tren mixto. Sus pasos, retumbando cada vez más lejanos, ***producían*** ecos profundos bajo tierra. (Doña Perfecta)
Before the caravan started moving, the train left, it was sliding through the track with the parsimony calmness of a mixed train. Its steps, echoing further away, produced deep echoes beneath the earth.

4. Frame of temporal reference: this variable includes absolute, intrinsic, relative, indeterminate, and irrelevant temporal references (Bender, Bennardo, & Beller, 2005; Evans, 2006; Schwenter & Torres

Cacoullos, 2008). An absolute temporal reference is expressed by a specific point in time, similar to an event on a calendar. The event of *la expedición fue el 22 de abril* 'the expedition was April 22' in (4.6a) is an absolute temporal reference because it is a specific date. An intrinsic temporal reference refers to an event that is temporally anchored to another event. This temporal reference occurs when the speaker is making mention of one event using a different one as the point of reference. For instance, (4.6b) has an intrinsic temporal reference in which *salieron del regno onde eran naturales* 'they left their kingdom' is temporally anchored to *e andudieron tanto en dies días* 'and they walked so much in ten days'. A relative temporal reference is an event that expresses the speaker's own relationship with the event. It indicates the speaker's own temporal perspective to the event (Evans, 2006). An example of a relative temporal reference is presented in (4.6c), in which the temporal reference of *dí* 'gave' is known to Erifila but the reader does not have that information. An indeterminate frame of reference is defined as a context without sufficient information to determine the temporal frame of reference. This type of temporal reference is exemplified in (4.6d), in which the reader is not given any other information about when Caballuco was in the faction. Finally, an irrelevant frame of reference is defined as a hypothetical or unreal situation (Schwenter & Torres Cacoullos, 2008). The fragment in (4.6e) illustrates an irrelevant temporal reference in which *estaba* 'he was' is irrelevant because it denotes an unreal event to the reader.

(4.6) a. Mi padre quiso pagar a Pepita el obsequio de la huerta y la convidó a visitar su quinta del Pozo de la Solana. La expedición *fue* el 22 de abril. No se me olvidará esta fecha. (Pepita Jiménez)
My father wanted to repay Pepita for the orchard gift and invited her to his country house at the Pozo de la Solana. The expedition was on April 22. I won't forget this date.

b. E levava en el cavallo en pos de sí el un fijuelo, e la dueña el otro. E **andudieron** tanto en dies días que **salieron** del regno onde eran naturales e entraron en otro reino… (Caballero de Zifar)
And he had on his horse behind him one of his children, and his wife the other one. And they walked so much in ten days that they went out of the kingdom from which they were native and entered another kingdom…

c. Yo arrepentida, Leonato? Eres menos de lo que eras? ¿quando yo el alma te *di*, no eras mi criado? (Los Locos de Valencia)
Sorry, am I, Leonato? Are you less of what you used to be? When I gave you my soul, were you not my servant?

d. No sé cómo no le ha oído usted nombrar en Madrid, porque es hijo de un famoso Caballuco que *estuvo* en la facción… (Doña Perfecta)
I don't know how you haven't heard his name in Madrid, because he is the son of the famous Caballuco that was in the group.

e. Estando en esto, llegó acaso a la venta un castrador de puercos, y así como llegó sonó su silbato de cañas cuatro o cinco veces, con lo cual acabó de confirmar Don Quijote que *estaba* en algún famoso castillo… (El Quijote)
Meanwhile, a person who castrates pigs arrived, and as he arrived, he blew his cane whistle four or five times, therefore Don Quijote ended up confirming that he was in some famous castle.

The frame of temporal reference was included because Schwenter and Torres Cacoullos (2008) showed that temporal reference is an important predictor when dealing with tempo-aspectual forms. Following Delgado-Díaz' (2014) results, it is expected that relative temporal reference will favor the imperfect because it describes the speaker's own temporal reference. In addition, it is anticipated that the preterit will be favored by absolute and intrinsic temporal references because it is likely viewed as a completed event. Furthermore, it is anticipated that an indeterminate temporal reference will not favor any form (preterit, imperfect, present perfect, imperfect progressive, and preterit progressive) because it is where variation can be best observed (Schwenter & Torres Cacoullos, 2008). However, it is possible that indeterminate temporal references favor the present perfect, in light of Schwenter and Torres Cacoullos' (2008) and Jara-Yupanqui's (2017) results. It may be inferred from the predictions on the preterit and imperfect that the imperfect progressive is favored by relative temporal while the preterit progressive is favored by absolute and intrinsic temporal references.

5. Temporal adverbs: this variable consists of durative, punctual, iterative, and no adverb. An example (4.7a) has a durative adverb *siempre* 'always', (4.7b) has a punctual adverb *una vez* 'always',

The study 69

(4.7c) has an iterative adverb *cada mañana* 'each morning', and (4.7d) has no adverb. The entire context was examined to determine whether an adverb influences multiple tokens. It is expected that ongoing adverbs trigger an ongoing interpretation, punctual adverbs a perfective function, and iterative adverbs a habitual meaning. This variable is important because the type of adverb will help determine the aspectual function of the tokens.

(4.7) a. El Vicario y yo permanecimos *siempre* serenos como las mulas, sin salir del paso y llevando a doña Casilda en medio. (Pepita Jiménez)
The vicar and I always remained serene like the mules, without leaving the trail and taking doña Casilda in the middle.

b. Oh amor, en que peligros vive, y muere, quien *una vez* probó la fuerza tuya! (Los Locos de Valencia)
Oh love, he lives in danger, and dies, anyone who tasted your strength!

c. E el uno dellos pensó esa noche de ir matar el otro en la mañana, ca sabía que *cada mañana* iva a marines, e fuelo a esperar tras la su puerta... (Caballero de Zifar)
And one of them thought that night on killing the other in the morning, because he knew that every morning he went to the docks, and he went and waited behind his door.

d. —Sin duda me han tomado por otro. —No...no...fuiste tú... Pero no vayas a ofenderte que aquí estamos entre amigos y personas de confianza. (Doña Perfecta)
—Without a doubt they have taken me for another. —No... No...it was you...But don't get offended because we are among friends and trustworthy people.

6. Specificity of the subject: this variable is a reinterpretation of the specificity of the event (Montrul & Slabakova, 2003; Rodríguez-Ramalle, 2005) which only includes the specificity of the subject (see section 1.2.1 in chapter 1 for an in-depth discussion regarding the specificity of the event). This variable includes two variants: specific and universal/non-specific subjects (Montrul & Slabakova, 2003; Rodríguez-Ramalle, 2005). Montrul and Slabakova (2003) and Rodríguez-Ramalle (2005) defined specific events as ones that have definite subjects. Definite subjects are those in which the agent can be identified with a specific person, animal, or object, for example,

yo 'I', *tú* 'you', *el niño* 'the boy', etc. The example (4.8a) was coded as specific because the subject of the verb *dixo* 'decir' is Rachel e Vida; in other words, it is identifiable. On the contrary, "generic" subjects cannot be identified with a specific person, animal, or object. These subjects are indefinite entities that make up a bigger class, such as humans, people, plants, animals, etc., following Rodríguez-Ramalle's (2005) and Montrul and Slabakova's (2003) definition of generic events. This includes passive/impersonal *se* (*se venden libros* 'books are sold'), or impersonal third person plural constructions (*robaron el banco* 'the bank was robbed') because they do not express a definable subject. An example of a non-specific subject is present in (4.8b) because the subject is *la gente* 'people'. It is expected that specific subjects will favor the preterit because they are more likely to express single completed events (Montrul & Slabakova, 2003). On the contrary, it is anticipated that generic subjects will favor the imperfect because they tend to express habitual events (Montrul & Slabakova, 2003). It is not clear how this variable will affect the past progressive forms since previous investigations have not included this variable.

(4.8) a. Dixo **Rachel e Vidas**: —Dárgelos hemos de grado.— (El Cantar del Mio Cid)
Rachel e Vidas said: —We will give them to him with pleasure—

b. Entraba y salía **la gente** en caballerías o a pie... (Doña Perfecta)
People were entering and leaving on horse or on foot...

7. Plurality of the direct object: this variable was coded for singular, plural, and no direct object. Example (4.9a) has a singular object *aquella esperanza* 'that hope', (4.9b) has a plural object *mis horar canónicas* 'my canonical hours', and (4.9c) was coded as no direct object because *salió* 'he went out' is an intransitive verb. This independent variable tries to capture the possible repetition of the event by observing the direct object. It is hypothesized that plural direct objects could favor a habitual function because they admit the repetition of the event (Schwenter & Torres Cacoullos, 2008). This implies that the imperfect would be favored by plural objects while the other forms (present perfect, preterit, imperfect progressive, and preterit progressive) would be favored by singular objects.

(4.9) a. ...no estaba ciego de amor ni de confianza descarté **aquella esperanza**, porque me entró mejor juego. (Los Locos de Valencia)
...I wasn't blind by love nor out of confidence I discarded that hope, it was because a better game entered me.
b. En substancia, todo es lo mismo. Yo también tenía **mis horas canónicas** en el cuartel de Guardias de Corps. (Pepita Jiménez)
In substance, everything is the same. I too had my canonical hours in the Corps Guards' headquarters.
c. El señor de la hueste armose muy toste en la tienda e **salió** en su cavallo, e un fijo con él... (Cabellero de Zifar)
The lord from the hueste armed himself very well in his tent and he left in his horse, and with one of his sons...

8. Animacy of the subject: this variable includes animate and inanimate subjects. For example, *seguía* 'he continued' in (4.10a) was coded as animate because the subject is Don Quijote. On the contrary, cases as *desencadenó* in (4.10b) were coded as inanimate because the subject is *la envidia* 'envy'. This variable was included because Comrie's (1976) definition of aspect includes the speaker's own point of view. Consequently, it is expected that animate subjects will favor the use of imperfect forms (simple and progressive) because it relates to the subject's own point of view. On the contrary, inanimate subjects will favor the preterit forms (simple and progressive) because they are less likely to express how they perceived the development of the event.

(4.10) a. ¿Quién ha puesto a vuestra merced de esta suerte? Pero **él**, seguía con su romance a cuanto le preguntaba. Viendo esto el buen hombre, lo mejor que pudo le quitó el peto y espaldar, para ver si tenía alguna herida; pero no vió sangre ni señal alguna. (El Quijote)
Who put you in this state? But he continued with his novel on everything he asked him. Seeing this, the good man took off his breastplate, to see if he had any injuries; but he did not see any sign of blood.
b. **La envidia** se desencadenó contra ella en los días que precedieron a la boda, y algunos meses después. (Pepita Jiménez)
Envy unleashed itself against her the days preceding the wedding, and some months after.

9. Grammatical person: this variable included first person, second person, and third person. The item *comencé* 'I started' in (4.11a) was coded as first person, *pudiste* 'you could' in (4.11b) was coded as second person, and *añadió* 'she added' and *comía* 'he was eating' in (4.11c) were both coded as third person. It is expected that the first person will favor the use of the imperfect. This hypothesis is based on the fact that the imperfect describes the internal distribution of the event (Comrie, 1976) and that grammatical person is linked to subjectivity of the event (Schwenter, 1994, Schwenter & Torres Cacoullos, 2008).

(4.11) a. ...la verdat me deve salvar, e con grant fuzia que en ella he non abré miedo, e iré con lo que *començé* cabo adelante, e non dexaré mi propósito començado» (Caballero de Zifar)
...the truth must save me, and I have so much hope in her that I will not be afraid, and I will go with what I have started, and I will not abandon my purpose that I have started»

b. ...Celia cruel, pues te *pudiste* trocar, podrá mi pecho fiel. (Los Locos de Valencia)
... cruel Celia, you could have changed, my faithful chest can.

c. —¡Pero cómo te pareces a tu padre! —*añadió* la señora, contemplando con verdadero
arrobamiento al joven mientras éste *comía*— (Doña Perfecta)
—You look just like your father!—added the lady, contemplating with complete ecstasy the young man while he was eating—

10. Lexical frequency of the item within the corpus was also examined. This factor was measured using raw and normalized frequency. Normalized frequency was included because it can be used to compare relative frequency across different size corpus. The formula used to normalize frequency is the following (McEnery & Wilson, 2001):

Number of occurrences of a token / Corpus size * 100

An example with *ser* 'to be' is presented in Table 4.2. *Ser* 'to be' was used 947 times in Medieval Spanish, 3,903 times in Golden Age Spanish, and 1,888 in Modern Spanish. These raw frequencies suggest that *ser* 'to

Table 4.2 Example of normalization formula with ser 'to be'

Frequency of ser according to the period	Corpus size	Formula	Proportional frequency
Medieval Spanish 947	60,000	947/60,000*100	1.6%
Golden Age Spanish 3,903	200,000	3903/200,000*100	2.0%
Modern Spanish 1,888	120,000	1,888/120,000*100	1.6%

be' was more frequent in the Golden Age and less frequent in Medieval Spanish. However, after normalizing the frequency it can be noted that the proportional frequency is the same in Medieval Spanish and Modern Spanish and slightly higher in Golden Age Spanish.

This factor was treated as a continuous variable and not as a discrete one (i.e., high, mid, low) to avoid making any ad hoc categorizations. Frequency is important because, according to Grammaticalization Theory, frequent lexical items are more susceptible to variation (Bybee, 2003a, 2003b, 2010; Bybee et al., 1994). Several predictions were drawn from this variable: first, it is expected that frequent tokens will be used with more forms; second, the preterit progressive will be used more frequently with frequent items.

11. Priming: this variable was coded as primed or non-primed. A token was coded as primed if the previous non-finite verb appeared in the same form. The fragment in (4.12a) exemplifies some primed items, in which *fizo* 'did' occurred after another preterit (*oyó* 'heard'). Similarly, in that same fragment, *vínose* 'came' and *díxole* 'told him/her' were considered primed since they occurred after another preterit (*se fue* 'he left'). On the contrary, the example (4.12b) demonstrates a non-primed item in which *había* 'there was' occurred after a simple present form (*se cree* 'it is believed'). It is worth mentioning that verbs in the infinitive were not considered when coding for this variable. Priming was included in the analysis because it facilitates access to "word, phrases, and constructions" (Bybee, 2007: 288) and it may also provide evidence for variable contexts. Specifically, this variable aims to identify what happens when several telic events (as tends to occur in literary works) are followed by an atelic event. Poplack and Tagliamonte (1999) found that priming has a strong effect in languages in which aspect

markings are optional, such as Nigerian Pidgin English. This could imply that contexts that allow variation between different forms may be susceptible to priming since multiple forms can express the same function. It is anticipated to find a priming effect in neutralized contexts because the aspectual meaning can be provided by different forms. On the contrary, priming will not have an effect in non-neutralized contexts because the aspectual meaning is conveyed by a given form. It is important to highlight the fact that this variable alone cannot determine which contexts are variable. This variable serves as a cue that helps to identify variable contexts.

(4.12) a. E el señor de casa desque lo oyó *fizo* como quien non dava nada por ello; e después que se fue el capellán, *vínose* para su amigo e *díxole* que se conortase, que de oro e plata atanto le daría quanto él quesiese... (Caballero de Zifar)
And the lord of the house since he heard him did as he did not care; and when the priest left, he went to his friend and told him comfort, that he would give him all the gold and silver he wanted...

b. Y fue, a lo que se cree, que en un lugar cerca del suyo *había* una moza labradora de muy buen parecer... (El Quijote)
And it was, as it is believed, that in a place near his there was a good-looking young female farmer...

The following variables were applied only to past progressive constructions (imperfect progressive and preterit progressive). Simple forms were coded as not applicable (N/A).

12. Co-occurrence with locative expressions: this variable was coded as co-occurrence with a locative expression and no locative expression. For example, the use of the imperfect progressive in (4.13a) co-occurred with the locative expression *a su lado* 'at his side'. On the contrary, the fragment in (4.13b) exemplifies a use of the imperfect progressive (*estávalos catando* 'he was observing them') without a locative expression. This variable was added because the progressive use of *estar* 'to be' appears first with a locative meaning and it was gradually lost in Spanish across time (Bybee et al., 1994; Torres Cacoullos, 2009, 2012). Therefore, it is expected that the past progressive forms are used less with locative expressions in Modern Spanish.

(4.13) a. Casi siempre *estaba* a su lado *acompañándole* y *mimándole* con singular cariño. (Pepita Jiménez)
Almost always she was at his side keeping him company and pampering him with the upmost care.

b. De los sos ojos tan fuertemientre llorando, tornava la cabeça e *estávalos catando*. Vío puertas abiertas e uços sin cañados, alcándaras vazías, sin pieles e sin mantos, e sin falcones e sin adtores mudados. (El Cantar del Mio Cid)
He was crying heavily from his eyes, he turned his head and he was observing them. He saw opened doors and doors without padlocks, empty hangers, without skins o cloaks, and without falcons and goshawks with changed feathers.

13. Adjacency: this variable refers to intervening material between the auxiliary verb and the gerund or participle (Torres Cacoullos, 2011: 152). This variable was coded as adjacent and non-adjacent. For example, the imperfect progressive in (4.14a) was coded as adjacent, while the imperfect progressive in (4.14b) was coded as non-adjacent. According to Grammaticalization Theory, it is expected that there will be more cases of non-adjacent uses of the past progressive forms (i.e., preterit progressive and imperfect progressive) in Medieval Spanish in contrast to Modern Spanish. This is because once the past periphrastic forms are grammaticalized they are viewed as one unit (Bybee & Torres Cacoullos, 2009). This implies that intervening material will appear less over the centuries.

(4.14) a. Y entre tanto que pugnaba por levantarse y no podía, *estaba diciendo*: non fuyáis, gente cobarde, gente cautiva, atended que no por culpa mía, sino de mi caballo, estoy aquí tendido. (El Quijote)
And while he was trying to get up and could not, he was saying, don't run away cowards, evil people, acknowledge that not by my fault, but my horse's, I am lying here.

b. ¿Y la señorita Rosarito que *estaba* ayer *disponiendo* el cuarto en que usted ha de vivir...? (Doña Perfecta)
And Miss Rosarito that was yesterday arranging the room that you are going to live in...

14. Association: this variable relates to the number of gerunds or participles associated to an auxiliary verb (Torres Cacoullos, 2011: 152). This variable was coded as one gerund, as in *estavan*

conbatiendo 'they were battling' in (4.15a), or multiple gerunds, as in *estaba durmiendo y soñando* 'he was sleeping and dreaming' in (4.15b). It is expected to find more instances of one gerund associated to an auxiliary verb in Modern Spanish because past periphrastic forms are viewed as a single unit (Bybee & Torres Cacoullos, 2009).

(4.15) a. E quando los sus cavalleros se ***estavan conbatiendo*** en el real con los de la hueste, enbió una doncella a los andamios, que parase mientes en cómo fazían. (Caballero de Zifar)
And when his knights were battling the people from the hueste where the king had his tent, he sent a damsel to the scaffolds, to stand there while they fought.

b. Y es lo bueno que no tenía los ojos abiertos, porque ***estaba durmiendo*** y ***soñando*** que estaba en batalla con el gigante... (El Quijote)
And the good thing is that he did not have his eyes opened, because he was sleeping and dreaming that he was battling the giant.

15. Fusion: this factor is related to placement of the object clitics (Torres Cacoullos, 2011: 152). This variable was coded as before the auxiliary verb, attached to the gerund, attached to the auxiliary verb, and no clitic present. The fragment in (4.16a) demonstrates the use of an imperfect progressive with the clitic before the auxiliary verb (*le estaba diciendo* 'I was telling you'). The example in (4.16b) shows a clitic attached at the auxiliary verb (*estávalos fablando* 'He was talking to them'). The fragment in (4.16c) exemplifies a clitic attached to the gerund (*estaba confuso mirándole* 'he was confused looking at him'). Finally, the example in (4.16d) exhibits a use of the imperfect progressive without a clitic (*estaban perpetuamente masticando* 'were perpetually chewing'). It is hypothesized that the clitic would appear more attached to the gerund or participle in Medieval Spanish, whereas it will appear more in front of the auxiliary verb in Modern Spanish (Torres Cacoullos, 2011). Bybee and Torres Cacoullos (2009) stated that the clitic tends to appear in front of the auxiliary verb as it becomes more grammaticalized (p.202).

(4.16) a. Ahora ***le estaba diciendo*** a Rosario que esta ciudad y esta casa me son tan agradables, que me gustaría vivir y morir aquí. (Doña Perfecta)

Now I was telling Rosario that this city and this house are so pleasing to me, that I would like to live and die here.
b. al Cid besáronle las manos. Sonrisós' mio Cid, *estávalos fablando*: —¡Ya don Rachel e Vidas, avédesme olbidado! (El cantar del Mio Cid)
Cid's hands were kissed. Mio Cid smiled at them, he was talking to them: — Don Rachel e Vidas has already obliged me.
c. El ventero que vió a su huésped a sus pies, y oyó semejantes razones, *estaba* confuso *mirándole*, sin saber qué hacerse ni decirle. (El Quijote)
The innkeeper saw his guest at his feet, and heard such reasons, he was confused looking at him, without knowing what to do or say.
d. …donde hacían tertulia diversas especies de progresistas rumiantes, que *estaban* perpetuamente *masticando* un tema sin fin; pero allí se aburrió más. (Doña Perfecta)
…where the social gathering was held diverse ruminant species, that were perpetually chewing an endless topic, but there he was even more bored.

4.2.3 Analysis

This section discusses the different analyses used in this book. A multiple response set was created to account for the fact that the independent variables have multiple levels. This methodology accounts for the fact that a form can express multiple aspectual meanings. Table 4.3 illustrates an example of the multiple response set, which exemplifies the coding of *podía* 'he could'. A "1" was entered under the imperfect column while "0" was entered in the other columns.

The data was analyzed using mixed effects model binary logistic regressions with SPSS. This type of analysis allowed entering fixed and random effect (Johnson, 2009; Tagliamonte, 2012). The variables discussed were entered as fixed factors while novel and items were entered as random effects. It is worth highlighting the fact that an independent logistic regression was done for each past-time expression. This means that the imperfect was selected as the dependent variable for one binary logistic regression, the preterit for another analysis, and so on. Independent logistic regressions were performed because the dependent variable (past form) contains at least five levels (not including other), thus providing a complex model for a multinomial

Table 4.3 Example coding of the multiple response set

Example	Imperfect	Preterit	Present perfect	Imperfect progressive	Preterit progressive	Other
Viendo, pues, que en efecto no **podía** menearse, acordó de acogerse a su ordinario remedio, que era pensar en algún paso de sus libros, y trájole su cólera a la memoria aquel de Baldovinos y del marqués de Mantua, cuando Carloto le dejó herido en la montaña... (El Quijote)	1	0	0	0	0	0

analysis. Finally, each period was analyzed separately to track its diachronic evolution.

Additionally, several conditional trees were done using Language Variation Suite (LVS) (Scrivner & Díaz-Campos, 2016) which "are a method of regression and classification based on binary recursive partitioning" (Levshina, 2015: 291) and it is useful in order to get a visual representation of the distribution of the data according to the significant factors. Additionally, this analysis is helpful to understand how the significant factors interact with each other and their constraint hierarchy (Baayen, 2008; Michnowicz, Despain, & Gorham, in press; Tagliamonte, 2012; Tagliamonte & Baayen, 2012).

Several cross-tabulations were performed when the data did not allow to run logistic regressions. Specifically, this descriptive analysis was done when there were few tokens of a past form or its distribution was skewed. These cross-tabulations aimed to describe the pattern of use of different past forms as well as uncovering trends in the data set.

5 Results

5.1 Introduction

This chapter presents the results of the diachronic analysis. Recall that the analysis yielded a total of 5,286 past expressions. Each time expression is discussed across Medieval Spanish, Golden Age Spanish, and Modern Spanish. Specifically, this chapter discusses the imperfect, the preterit, the present perfect, and the progressive forms. The result sections are guided by the mixed-model logistic regressions or by trends found in the data whenever statistical analyses were not possible.

5.2 The imperfect

This section discusses the results pertaining the imperfect in Medieval Spanish, Golden Age Spanish, and Modern Spanish. Table 5.1 illustrates the distribution of the imperfect in each period. It is worth noticing that the frequency of use increased from Medieval Spanish to Golden Age Spanish and from Golden Age Spanish to Modern Spanish.

Several mixed-model logistic regressions were performed to determine which factor predicts the imperfect in each period. Table 5.2 illustrates the results of these analyses, in which gray areas highlight significant factors. The first column with each period includes F value, the second column presents the degrees of freedom, and the last column illustrates the significance value. Empty cells mean that the factor was not included in the analysis due to skewed data. These analyses revealed that aspectual function, type of information, and priming were significant in the three periods. On the contrary, lexical semantics was not significant in Medieval Spanish, but it was found significant in Golden Age Spanish. This factor was not entered in Modern Spanish due to skewed data. Regarding frame of temporal reference, this factor was not entered in Medieval Spanish, it was not significant in Golden Spanish, but it was significant in Modern Spanish.

80   Results

Table 5.1 Distribution of the imperfect across centuries

	Medieval Spanish	Golden Age Spanish	Modern Spanish	Total
Imperfect	420 (21.9%)	641 (33.4%)	858 (44.7%)	1,919 (100%)

Conditional trees of each period are analyzed to identify the constraint hierarchy of the factors that predict the use of the imperfect. Figure 5.1 illustrates the conditional tree for the imperfect in Medieval Spanish. Recall that this analysis determines how the significant factors interact with each other as well as constraint hierarchy (Michnowicz et al., in press; Scrivner & Díaz-Campos, 2016; Tagliamonte, 2012). The node numbers represent the constraint hierarchy, each node illustrates a significant split at the .05 level, and the bar plots at the bottom show the proportion of the imperfect within each condition (Levshina, 2015). Figure 5.1 shows that the most important factor is aspectual function followed by type of information and priming. Additionally, the conditional tree found that perfective events differed from habitual, indeterminate, and progressive contexts. Moreover, habitual and progressive contexts differed from indeterminate ones in foreground information. The imperfect tends to be used with background information, as shown in node 3. Node 5 illustrates that the imperfect with foreground information is used with habitual and progressive aspectual functions. It can be noted on the right side of the tree that perfective events were influenced by priming, in which primed contexts were affected by the type of information while non-primed contexts were not. Node 11 shows that the imperfect is not used with primed contexts expressing foreground information.

Figure 5.2 illustrates the conditional tree regarding the factors that influence the use of the imperfect in Golden Age Spanish. It can be noted that aspectual function was the most important factor followed by lexical semantics, priming, and type of information. Additionally, this analysis revealed that habitual, progressive, and indeterminate events differed from perfective ones. Node 13 shows that the imperfect had a low frequency of use in perfective contexts. Habitual, progressive, and indeterminate contexts were influenced by lexical semantics while perfective contexts were not. Node 2 shows that perception verbs differed from accomplishments, achievements, activities, cognitive, and states while node 3 illustrates that accomplishments, achievements, and activities were influenced by priming. On the contrary, cognitive and stative verbs were influenced by aspectual function. Node 7 shows

Table 5.2 Mixed-effects logistic regressions models for the imperfect according to period

Factor	Medieval Spanish			Golden Age Spanish			Modern Spanish		
	F	df	Sig.	F	df	Sig.	F	df	Sig.
Corrected Model	340.827	1,548	.000	12.984	1,776	.000	43.834	1,918	.000
Aspectual Function	340.827	1,548	.000	95.095	1,776	.000	167.308	1,918	.000
Lexical semantic	1.589	1,548	.208	5.363	1,776	.000			
Type of information	202.091	1,548	.000	7.076	1,776	.008	27.678	1,918	.000
Frame of temporal reference				2.115	1,776	.077	3.140	1,918	.014
Temporal adverb									
Specificity of the subject	2.300	1,548	.130	0.495	1,776	.482	0.247	1,918	.787
Plurality of the direct object	0.020	1,548	.887	0.058	1,776	.994			
Grammatical person				1.796	1,776	.166			
Animacy	2.401	1,548	.121	0.560	1,776	.454	0.073	1,918	.619
Priming	60.226	1,548	.000	12.523	1,776	.000	5.189	1,918	.023
Raw frequency			.594			.441			.487
Normalized frequency			.594			.441			.487

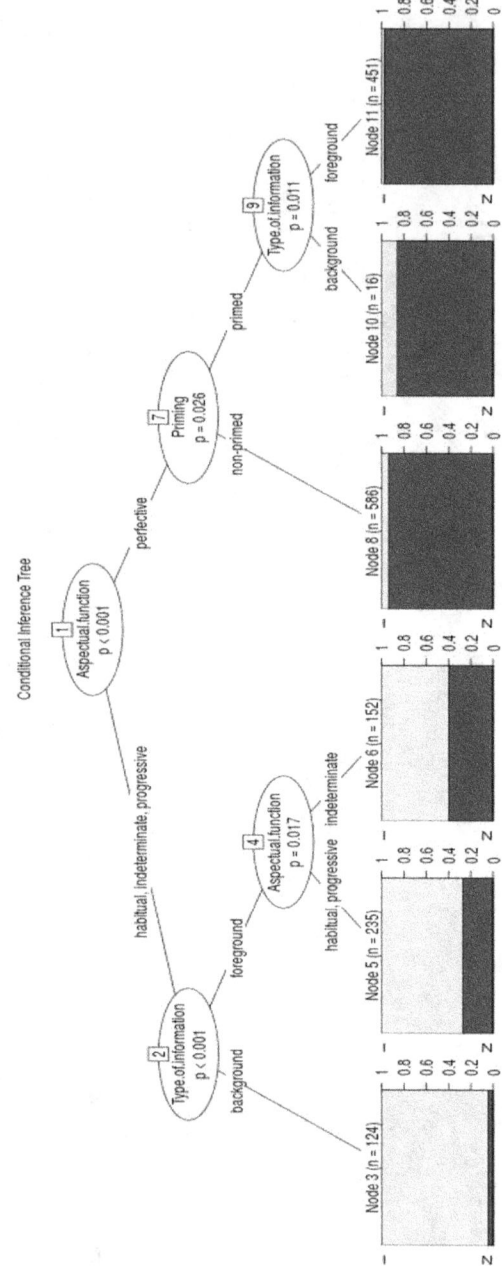

Figure 5.1 Conditional tree of the factors that influence the imperfect in Medieval Spanish

Results 83

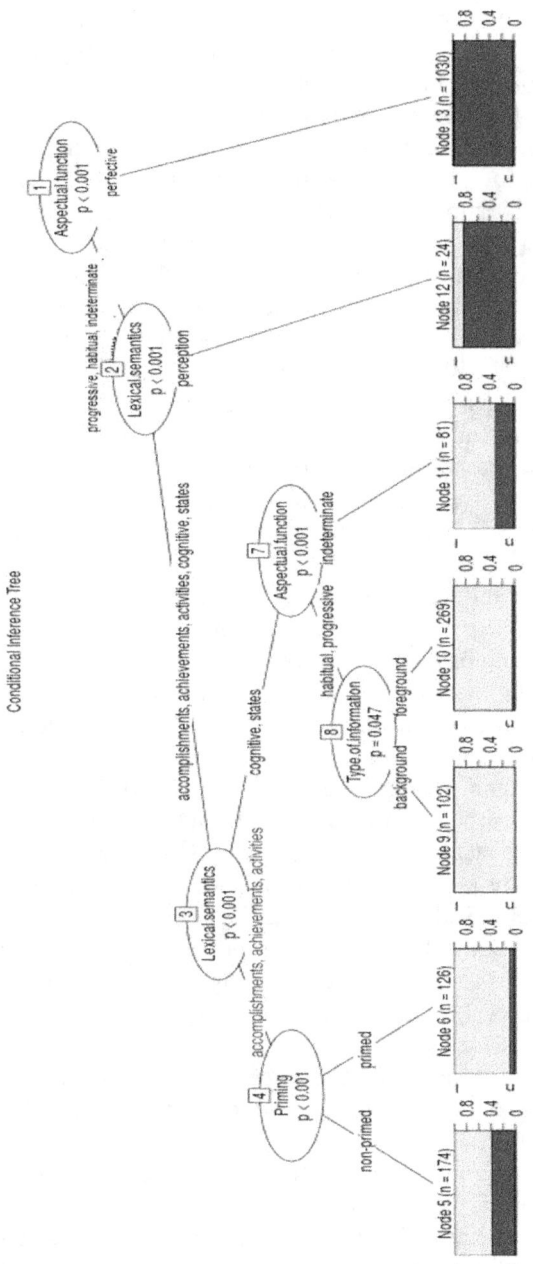

Figure 5.2 Conditional tree of the factors that influence the imperfect in Golden Age Spanish

that habitual and progressive events were influenced by the type of information while indeterminate contexts were not. The imperfect was used more frequently with habitual and progressive events expressing foreground and background information, as illustrated in nodes 9 and 10.

Figure 5.3 illustrates the conditional tree of the factors that influence the imperfect in Modern Spanish. This analysis found that the most important factor was aspectual function followed by type of information, frame of temporal reference, and priming. In addition, this analysis revealed that habitual, progressive, and indeterminate contexts differed from perfective contexts. Node 2 illustrates that foreground information was influenced by frame of temporal reference while background information was not. Node 3 shows that the imperfect was used more frequently with habitual, indeterminate, and progressive contexts expressing background information. Moreover, node 4 shows that indeterminate, intrinsic, and irrelevant temporal references were influenced by priming while absolute and relative temporal references were not. The conditional tree illustrates that the imperfect was used more frequently with progressive, habitual, and indeterminate contexts. It can be observed on the right side of the conditional tree that perfective contexts were influenced by type of information. Finally, node 10 illustrates that the imperfect was used more frequently with perfective events expressing background information.

Table 5.3 summarizes the results of the conditional trees; it illustrates the significant factors and constraint hierarchy in each period. It can be observed that the most important factor in Medieval Spanish, Golden Age Spanish, and Modern Spanish was aspectual function. Type of information was the second most significant factor in Medieval Spanish, while it was the last factor in Golden Age Spanish and the second most important factor in Modern Spanish. Lexical semantics was not significant in Medieval Spanish, but it was the second most important factor in Golden Age Spanish. Lexical semantics was not included in the statistical analysis in Modern Spanish. Priming was the third most important factor in Medieval Spanish and Golden Age Spanish, while it was the least significant factor in Modern Spanish. Finally, frame of temporal reference was not included in Medieval Spanish, it was not significant in Golden Age Spanish, while it was the third most important factor in Modern Spanish.

The distribution of the imperfect is analyzed according to each significant factor. Table 5.4 illustrates the distribution of the imperfect according to aspectual function. This table indicates that the imperfect was used more frequently to express a progressive aspectual function in the three time periods. It is worth highlighting that this past form was

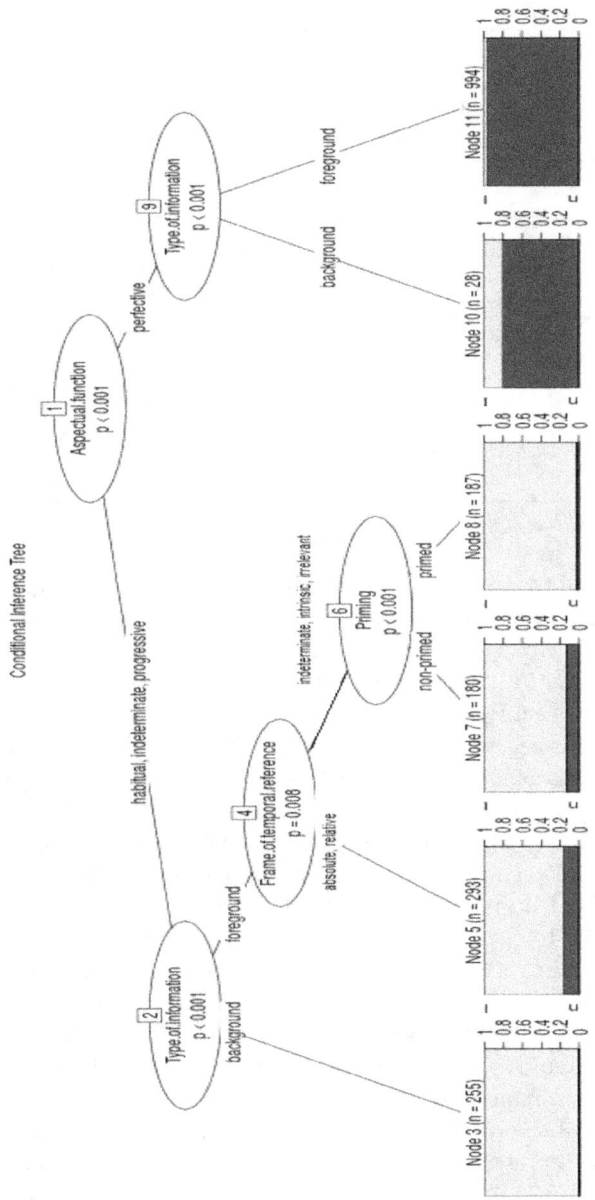

Figure 5.3 Conditional tree of the factors that influence the imperfect in Modern Spanish

Table 5.3 Constraint hierarchy of the imperfect according to period

Medieval Spanish	Golden Age Spanish	Modern Spanish
Aspectual function Type of information Priming	Aspectual function Lexical semantics Priming Type of information	Aspectual function Type of information Frame of temporal reference Priming

Table 5.4 Aspectual function of the imperfect according to period

Period	Habitual	Progressive	Perfective	Indeterminate	Total
Medieval Spanish	29 (6.9%)	244 (58.1%)	41 (9.8%)	106 (25.2%)	420 (100%)
Golden Age Spanish	48 (7.5%)	443 (69.1%)	11 (1.7%)	139 (21.7%)	641 (100%)
Modern Spanish	50 (5.8%)	593 (69.1%)	28 (3.3%)	187 (21.8%)	858 (100%)

scarcely used to express a habitual function. In fact, the imperfect was used more frequently to express a perfective function than a habitual function in Medieval Spanish. The low frequency of the imperfect with a habitual aspectual function may be because literary works, at least the ones analyzed, do not tend to include many habitual contexts. However, it is necessary to include other literary works to support this hypothesis. In general, these results support previous investigations on the imperfect which stated that it is mainly used to express progressive and habitual aspectual functions (Ayres, 2009; Baker & Quesada, 2011; Bello, 1847; Bybee et al., 1994; Cipria & Roberts, 2000; Comrie, 1976; Delgado-Díaz, in press; Lamanna, 2008, 2012; Montrul & Slabakova, 2003; RAE, 1973, 2010; Rodríguez-Ramalle, 2005). On the contrary, the results indicate that the imperfect was scarcely used to express a perfective function in the three time periods. Furthermore, the frequency of the imperfect with a perfective function decreased from Medieval Spanish to Golden Age Spanish, but there was a slight increase from Golden Age Spanish to Modern Spanish. Similar results were found by Delgado-Díaz (in press) in which the imperfect was used in limited contexts to express a perfective function in Puerto Rican Spanish. The fragment in (5.1) illustrates an imperfect with a perfective function, in which *avíamos* 'we had' was coded as perfective because it is a single and completed event in the past.

(5.1) E porque creades que es así, preguntad a tales omes buenos, e ellos vos dirán de cómo anoche tarde *avíamos* nuestras palabras muy feas yo e él, e ellos nos despartieron. (Caballero de Zifar)
And because you believe that it is like that, ask those good men, and they will tell you that late last night he and I had an argument, and they separated us.

The distribution of the imperfect according to type of information and aspectual function is examined since the conditional trees found that these factors interact with each other in the three periods. Table 5.5 shows that the imperfect was used frequently in background information with a progressive aspectual function, as illustrated in example (5.2a). This finding may be because background information provides descriptions (Hopper, 1979), which tend to be progressive. This result supports previous investigations on the imperfect, which found that it is mainly used to express background information (Delgado-Díaz, 2018b; Gonzales, 1995; Gutiérrez-Araus, 1998; Silva-Corvalán, 1983; Soto, 2011; Reyes, 1990; Weinrich, 1968; Westfall, 1995). However, the imperfect was used frequently with foreground information, as illustrated in example (5.2b), similarly to Delgado-Díaz' (2018b) findings in Buenos Aires Spanish. Consequently, these results suggest that the Discourse Hypothesis (Hopper, 1979) is not categorical, but rather, it describes a tendency in which the imperfect is used more frequently to express background information (Bardovi-Harlig, 2000). Interestingly, the imperfect with a perfective aspectual tended to appear expressing foreground information.

Table 5.5 Distribution of the imperfect according to type of information and period

		Habitual	Progressive	Perfective	Indeterminate	Total
Medieval Spanish	Foreground	20 (6.7%)	150 (50.2%)	38 (12.7%)	91 (30.4%)	299 (100%)
	Background	9 (7.4%)	94 (77.7%)	3 (2.5%)	15 (12.4%)	121 (100%)
Golden Age Spanish	Foreground	39 (7.8%)	327 (65.1%)	11 (2.2%)	125 (24.9%)	502 (100%)
	Background	9 (6.5%)	116 (83.5%)	0	14 (10.1%)	139 (100%)
Modern Spanish	Foreground	35 (5.8%)	402 (66.9%)	23 (3.8%)	141 (23.5%)	601 (100%)
	Background	15 (5.8%)	191 (74.3%)	5 (1.9%)	46 (17.9%)	257 (100%)

(5.2) a. ...y una sobrina que no *llegaba* a los veinte... (El Quijote)
...and niece that wasn't even twenty...
   b. ...los otros que estavan enderredor de la villa se *armavan* quanto podían e van
corriendo contra las tiendas del señor de la hueste do son aquellos polvos. (Caballero de Zifar)
...the others that were near the village armed themselves how they could, and they went running toward the tents of the army's lord, where the dust is.

Table 5.6 illustrates the distribution of the imperfect according to priming. It can be noted that the imperfect was used more frequently in non-primed contexts, as illustrated in (5.3a). This may suggest that the imperfect was used to express an overt aspectual function (Poplack & Tagliamonte, 1999). However, the use of the imperfect in primed contexts increased through time. The fragment in (5.3b) illustrates three cases of the imperfect in primed contexts. It should be highlighted that, according to the conditional trees, priming is influenced by different factors in these periods. For instance, it is affected by aspectual function in Medieval Spanish, with lexical semantics in Golden Age Spanish, and with temporal frame of reference in Modern Spanish.

(5.3) a. Ya he dicho que *era* tío de la Pepita. (Pepita Jiménez)
I already said that he was Pepita's uncle.
   b. No se le ocultaba que si bien no *era* marido, ni hermano, ni pariente de Pepita, *podía* sacar la cara por ella como caballero; pero *veía* el escándalo que esto causaría cuando no había allí ningún profano que defendiese a Pepita, antes bien, todos reían al Conde la gracia. (Pepita Jiménez)
It was no hidden fact that if I was not husband, brother, or relative of Pepita, I could not defend her honor like a gentleman; I saw he scandal that this would cause when there wasn't any profane person that would defend Pepita, on the contrary, everyone was laughing at the Count's jokes.

Table 5.6 Distribution of the imperfect according to priming and period

	Primed	*Non-primed*	*Total*
Medieval Spanish	158 (37.6%)	262 (62.4%)	420 (100%)
Golden Age Spanish	276 (43.1%)	365 (56.9%)	641 (100%)
Modern Spanish	418 (48.7%)	440 (51.3%)	858 (100%)

Finally, lexical semantics was significant in Golden Age Spanish. This factor is illustrated according to aspectual function since the conditional tree found that both these factors interacted with each other. Table 5.7 shows that the imperfect was used more frequently with a progressive function with all semantic classes. Although, it can be observed that the imperfect with a progressive function was used more frequently with stative verbs, as illustrated in (5.4). Additionally, the limited cases of the imperfect with a perfective function appeared with accomplishment and achievement verbs.

(5.4) Y es cierto que entonces desmayé de tal manera, que mas que el Rey *estaba* ciado y yerto salí por una encrucijada afuera... (Los Loco de Valencia)
And it is true that then I fainted, and that the King was stiff and I exited outside through a crossroad...

5.3 The preterit

This section discusses the results of the preterit. Table 5.8 illustrates the raw frequencies of the preterit in the three periods. It can be noted that its frequency of use is relatively similar across centuries.

The results from the mixed-effects logistic regressions are presented in Table 5.9, in which the shaded cells highlight the significant factors. It can be noted that aspectual function was significant in the three time

Table 5.7 Distribution of the imperfect in Golden Age Spanish according to the lexical semantic of the verb

	Habitual	*Progressive*	*Perfective*	*Indeterminate*	*Total*
States	9 (2.3%)	329 (85.9%)	0	45 (11.7%)	383 (100%)
Activities	8 (17.4%)	24 (52.2%)	0	14 (30.4%)	46 (100%)
Accomplishments	24 (15.9%)	61 (40.4%)	9 (6%)	57 (37.7%)	151 (100%)
Achievements	7 (22.6%)	9 (29%)	2 (6.5%)	13 (41.9%)	31 (100%)
Cognitive	0.0%	17 (65.4%)	0	9 (34.6%)	26 (100%)
Perception	0	3 (75%)	0	1 (25%)	4 (100%)

Table 5.8 Distribution of the preterit across centuries

	Medieval Spanish	*Golden Age Spanish*	*Modern Spanish*	*Total*
Preterit	1,068 (34.4%)	1,025 (33%)	1,011 (32.6%)	3,104 (100%)

Table 5.9 Mixed-effects logistic regressions models for the preterit according to period

Factor	Medieval Spanish			Golden Age Spanish			Modern Spanish		
	F	df	Sig.	F	df	Sig.	F	df	Sig.
Corrected Model	28.446	1,537	.000	24.801	1,781	.000	48.604	1,918	.000
Aspectual Function	109.687	1,537	.000	126.606	1,781	.000	178.038	1,918	.000
Lexical semantic	1.386	1,537	.230	0.519	352	.762			
Type of information	21.184	1,537	.000	1.448	1,781	.229	14.237	1,918	.000
Frame of temporal reference				1.959	1,781	.098	2.348	1,918	.052
Temporal adverb									
Specificity of the subject	0.966	1,537	.326	5.010	1,781	.025	0.668	1,918	.414
Plurality of the direct object	0.599	1,537	.549	0.465	883	.628			
Grammatical person				6.693	1,781	.001			
Animacy	0.741	1,537	.389	0.319	1,781	.572	0.047	1,918	8.28
Priming	32.362	1,537	.000	0.873	1,781	.350	0.514	1,918	.473
Raw frequency			.125			.254			.708
Normalized frequency			.125			.254			.708

Results 91

periods. Additionally, type of information was significant in Medieval Spanish and Modern Spanish. Grammatical person and specificity of the subject were significant in Golden Age Spanish, while priming was significant in Medieval Spanish.

A series of conditional trees are examined to determine the constraint hierarchy of these factors and how they interact with each other. Figure 5.4 illustrates the conditional tree of the factors that influence the preterit in Medieval Spanish. It can be noted that the most important factor is aspectual function followed by type of information and priming, which interacted with each other. For instance, nodes 11 and 13 show that perfective aspectual function is influenced by priming and type of information. The preterit is used more frequently with a perfective function in primed contexts, and with foreground information. Similarly, nodes 2 and 8 illustrate that the preterit was used more frequently with indeterminate aspectual function and primed contexts. Finally, nodes 3 and 5 demonstrate that the preterit with a habitual and progressive function was influenced by type of information and priming. More precisely, the preterit was used slightly more frequently with a habitual and progressive function with foreground information and primed contexts in contrast to background information and non-primed contexts.

The conditional tree in Figure 5.5 illustrates the factors that influence the use of the preterit in Golden Age Spanish. It can be noted that aspectual function was the most important factor followed by grammatical person and specificity of the subject. Furthermore, node 9 illustrates that the preterit with a perfective function was influenced by grammatical person, in which the second person behaved differently than first and third persons. There were less uses of the preterit with a perfective function in the second grammatical person. The preterit with a perfective function was used more frequently in the third grammatical person with specific subjects. Additionally, node 12 shows that third and first persons were influenced by specific events. Node 2 illustrates that habitual and progressive events behaved differently than indeterminate aspectual contexts. In fact, it can be noted in node 6 that there were more cases of the preterit in indeterminate contexts with first person subjects. Finally, node 3 indicates that there were slightly more uses of the preterit with progressive or habitual aspectual functions with second and first grammatical persons, as opposed to the third person.

Finally, Figure 5.6 illustrated the conditional tree regarding the factors that influence the use of the preterit in Modern Spanish. It can be noted that aspectual function is the most important factor followed by type of information. Furthermore, node 9 illustrates that the preterit

92 *Results*

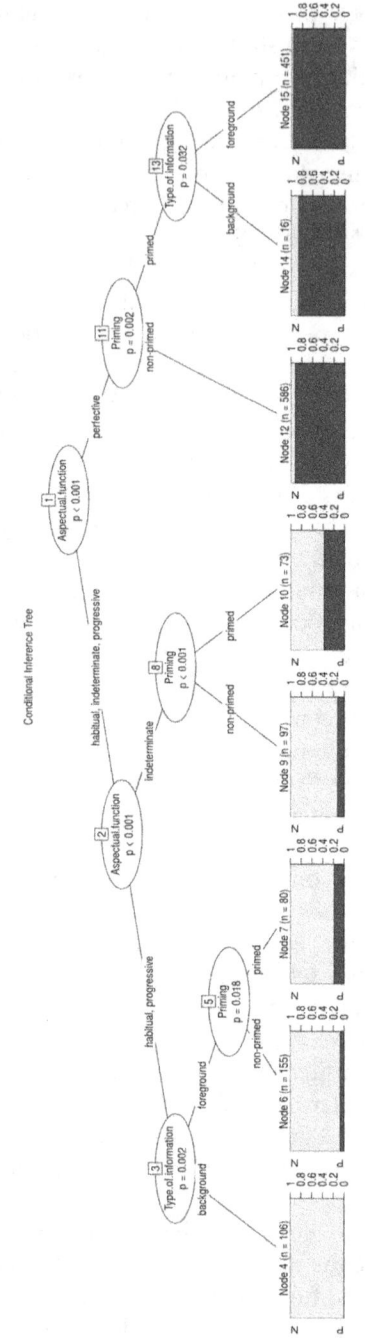

Figure 5.4 Conditional tree of the factors that influence the preterit in Medieval Spanish

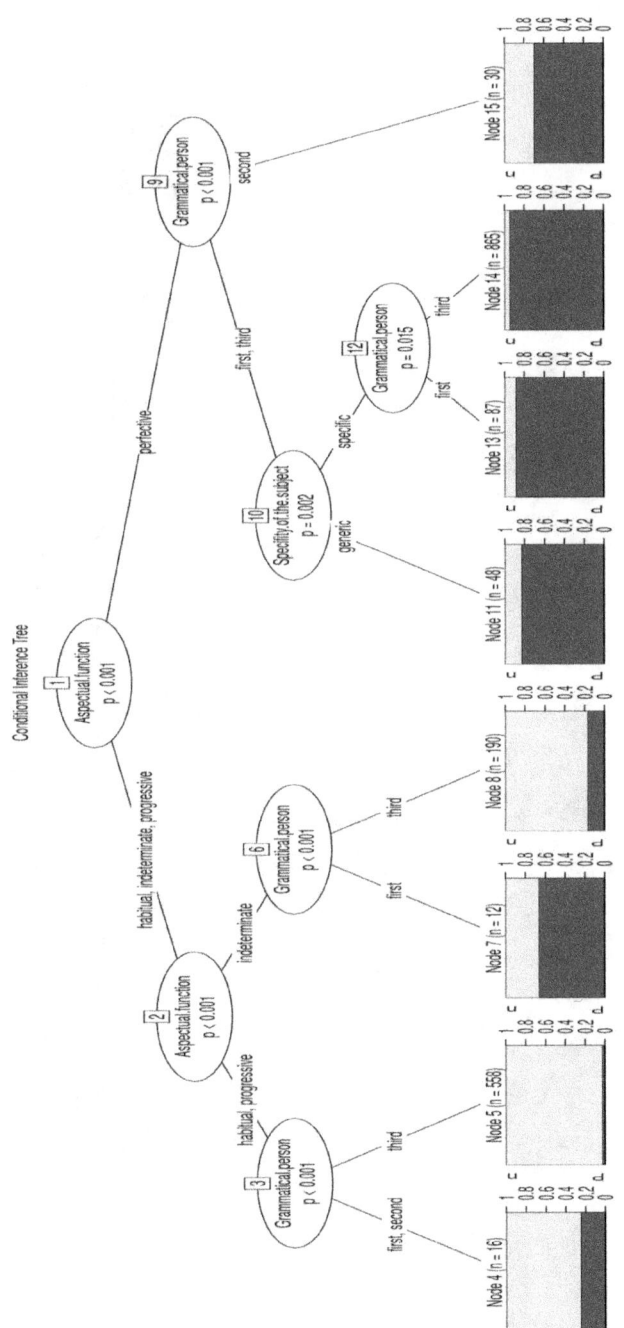

Figure 5.5 Conditional tree of the factors that influence the preterit in Golden Age Spanish

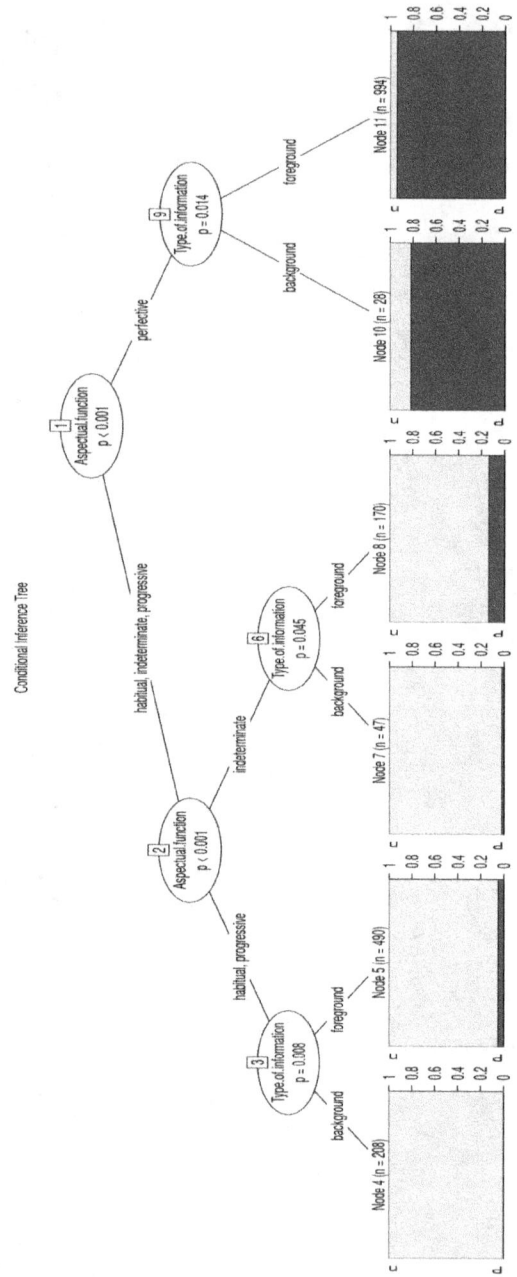

Figure 5.6 Conditional tree of the factors that influence the preterit in Modern Spanish

with a perfective function was used more frequently with foreground information. In addition, nodes 3 and 6 demonstrate that the preterit with progressive and habitual aspectual function, and in indeterminate contexts, was used more frequently with foreground information.

Table 5.10 presents a summary of the findings of the conditional trees regarding the preterit. It can be noted that aspectual function was the most important factor in the three periods. Type of information was the second most important factor in Medieval Spanish and Modern Spanish. However, this factor was not significant in Golden Age Spanish. Priming was the third most significant factor in Medieval Spanish. In Golden Age Spanish, grammatical person was the second most important factor followed by specificity of the subject.

The distribution of the preterit is discussed according to the results of the mixed-model logistic regressions and the conditional trees. Table 5.11 illustrates the distribution of the preterit according to type of information and aspectual function in the three periods. It can be noted that this aspectual form was used more frequently with a perfective function in foreground information. Example (5.5a) illustrates a preterit *pronunció* 'she pronounced' with a perfective function and expressing foreground information. This finding supports the previous account on the preterit, which stated that it is mainly used to express a

Table 5.10 Constraint hierarchy of the preterit according to period

Medieval Spanish	Golden Age Spanish	Modern Spanish
Aspectual function	Aspectual function	Aspectual function
Type of information	Grammatical person	Type of information
Priming	Specificity of the subject	

Table 5.11 Distribution of the preterit across centuries according to type of information and aspectual function

		Habitual	Progressive	Perfective	Indeterminate	Total
Medieval Spanish	Foreground	2 (.2%)	26 (2.5%)	979 (93.6%)	39 (3.9%)	1,046 (100%)
	Background	0	1 (4.3%)	20 (87%)	2 (8.7%)	23 (100%)
Golden Age Spanish	Foreground	3 (.3%)	16 (1.6%)	928 (94.1%)	39 (4%)	986 (100%)
	Background	0	1 (2.6%)	36 (92.3%)	2 (5.1%)	39 (100%)
Modern Spanish	Foreground	1 (.1%)	23 (2.3%)	938 (95.1%)	24 (2.4%)	986 (100%)
	Background	0	1 (4%)	23 (92%)	1 (4%)	25 (100%)

perfective function (Baker & Quesada, 2011; Delgado-Díaz, in press; Howe & Schwenter, 2008; Schwenter & Torres Cacoullos, 2008; RAE, 1973, 2010; Westfall, 1995, 2003). Additionally, the results indicate that the preterit could express other aspectual functions when it expresses foreground information, as documented by Brucart (2003), Champion (1973), and Delgado-Díaz (in press). The use of *permanecimos* 'we remained', in example (5.5b), was coded as progressive since it signals an ongoing event and it also provides foreground information. Delgado-Díaz (in press) found similar results in Puerto Rican Spanish, in which the preterit was used in limited cases to express progressiveness and habituality. Finally, this example illustrates that the preterit was scarcely used to express background information, which supports the Discourse Hypothesis (Hopper, 1979) and previous studies (Bardovi-Harlig, 2000; Delgado-Díaz, 2018b; Silva-Corvalán, 1983; Weinrich, 1968; Westfall, 1995). However, there are few cases of the preterit with a perfective aspectual function expressing background information, as shown in (5.5c). In this example, *indiqué* 'I pointed out' was coded as background information because it provides a commentary. These results suggest that the Discourse Hypothesis (Hopper, 1979) is predictive hypothesis rather than categorical (Bardovi-Harlig, 2000).

(5.5) a. Al ser saludada por su primo, se puso como la grana y sólo ***pronunció*** algunas palabras torpes. (Doña Perfecta)
Being greeted by her cousin, she turned like a pomegranate and only pronounced some clumsy words.

b. El Vicario y yo ***permanecimos*** siempre serenos como las mulas, sin salir del paso y llevando a doña Casilda en medio. (Pepita Jiménez)
The Vicar and I always remained calm like the mules, without losing pace and taking doña Casilda in the middle.

c. Todas las noches, de nueve a doce, tenemos, como ya ***indiqué*** a usted, tertulia en casa de Pepita. (Pepita Jiménez)
Every night, from nine to twelve, we have, like I already pointed out to you, social gatherings in Pepita's house.

The distribution of the preterit in Medieval Spanish is illustrated according to aspectual function, priming, and type of information in Table 5.12. Recall that these are the significant factors and they influence each other. It can be observed that the preterit was used more frequently with a perfective function and expressing foreground information. Additionally, the preterit with a perfective function expressing

Table 5.12 Distribution of the preterit according to aspectual function, priming and type of information in Medieval Spanish

		Habitual	Progressive	Perfective	Indeterminate	Total
Primed	Foreground	1 (.2%)	15 (3.1%)	441 (91.1%)	27 (5.6%)	484 (100%)
	Background	0	0	14 (93%)	1 (6.7%)	15 (100%)
Non-primed	Foreground	1 (.2%)	11 (2%)	538 (95.7%)	12 (2.1%)	562 (100%)
	Background	0	1 (12.5%)	6 (75%)	1 (12.5%)	8 (100%)

foreground information was used slightly more in non-primed contexts than in primed contexts. This finding may suggest that the preterit expresses an overt aspectual function (Poplack & Tagliamonte, 1999). Examples (5.6a–b) illustrate cases of the preterit with a progressive function expressing foreground information; (5.6a) is a non-primed context while (5.6b) is in a primed context.

(5.6) a. **Salieron** de Alcocer a una priessa much estraña. (El Cantar del Mio Cid)
They exited Alcocer with a strange hurry.
b. E desque los parientes de la moça lo sopieron, toviéronse por desonrados e **enbiáronle** a desafiar, e **corrieron** con él muy grant tienpo. (Caballero de Zifar)
And since the girl's parents knew it, they were dishonored and they were ordered to defy, and they ran for a very long time.

Table 5.13 illustrates the distribution of the preterit in Golden Age Spanish according to specificity of the subject, grammatical person, and aspectual function. It can be noted that the preterit was used more frequently with a perfective function, specific subjects, and with third person subjects, which supports Montrul and Slabakova's (2003) and Rodríguez-Ramalle's (2005) predictions. Example (5.7a) illustrates a use of the preterit with a specific third person subject. Additionally, the preterit with progressive and indeterminate aspectual functions was used slightly more frequently with third person and specific subjects. Example (5.7b) shows a use of the preterit with a progressive aspectual function and a specific third person subject. In this example, *anduvo* 'to walk' (it roughly translates to 'to be' in this context) was coded as progressive because it is modified by *un tiempo* 'for some time'. These results suggest that the prototypical context of the preterit in Golden Age Spanish is perfective contexts with specific third person subjects.

Table 5.13 Distribution of the preterit in Golden Age Spanish according to specificity of the subject, grammatical person, and aspectual function

Specificity of the subject	Grammatical person	Habitual	Progressive	Perfective	Indeterminate	Total
Specific	First person	0	3 (3.4%)	77 (87.5%)	8 (9.1%)	88 (100%)
	Second person	0	1 (4.5%)	21 (95.5%)	0	22 (100%)
	Third person	3 (.3%)	11 (1.3%)	826 (94.9%)	30 (3.4%)	870 (100%)
Non-specific	First person	0	0	0	0	0
	Second person	0	0	0	0	0
	Third person	0	2 (4.4%)	40 (88.9%)	3 (6.7%)	45 (100%)

Additionally, these results may indicate that the preterit may express a different aspectual function (i.e., progressive, habitual, or indeterminate) with specific third person subjects.

(5.7) a. Se *armó* de todas sus armas... (El Quijote)
He armed himself with all his weapons.
b. Y fue, a lo que se cree, que en un lugar cerca del suyo había una moza labradora de muy buen parecer, de quien él un tiempo *anduvo* enamorado, aunque según se entiende, ella jamás lo supo ni se dió cata de ello. (El Quijote)
And it was, as it was believed to be, that in a place near his own place there was a farmer woman, that he was in love with her for some time, even though as it is believed, she never knew it nor she found out.

5.4 Present perfect

This section discusses the results regarding the present perfect. Recall that the present perfect was included in the analysis when it expressed a perfective function because perfect aspectual function falls outside the scope of the present investigation. Consequently, few cases of the present perfect were included in the analysis, which contrast with other investigations on the present perfect (Copple, 2011; Hernández, 2004, 2008; Schwenter & Torres Cacoullos, 2008, among others). Table 5.14 illustrates the cases of the present perfect across centuries. It can be observed that the present perfect with a perfective function increased from Medieval Spanish to Golden Age Spanish. However, its frequency decreased from Golden Age Spanish to Modern Spanish. It is possible that the relative high frequency of the present perfect in Golden Age Spanish is due to dialogs in *Los Locos de Valencia*. There were 51 cases of the present perfect with a perfective function in Golden Age Spanish, of which 38 cases were found in *Los Locos de Valencia*. This could imply that the present perfect with a perfective aspectual function is best found in dialogs, rather than in prose.

Table 5.14 Distribution of the present perfect across centuries

	Medieval Spanish	*Golden Age Spanish*	*Modern Spanish*	*Total*
Present perfect	5 (6.1%)	51 (62.2%)	26 (31.7%)	82 (100%)

Table 5.15 Distribution of the present perfect across centuries according to lexical semantics

	States	Activities	Accomplishments	Achievements	Cognitive	Perception	Total
Medieval Spanish	1 (20%)	0	0	4 (80%)	0	0	5 (100%)
Golden Age Spanish	5 (9.8%)	0	23 (45.1%)	21 (41.2%)	1 (2%)	1 (2%)	51 (100%)
Modern Spanish	2 (7.7%)	1 (3.8%)	13 (50%)	8 (30.8%)	1 (3.8%)	1 (3.8%)	26 (100%)

The overall low frequency of the present perfect with a perfective function does not allow us to perform statistical analyses; consequently, this section presents trends found in the data. For instance, Table 5.15 illustrates the distribution of the present perfect according to lexical semantics. It can be observed that the present perfect with a perfective function was used more frequently with accomplishment and achievement verbs. Example (5.8a) illustrates a present perfect with an achievement verb and example (5.8b) illustrates an accomplishment verb. Additionally, these results suggest that the present perfect with a perfective function emerged from achievement verbs in Medieval Spanish and spread to accomplishment verbs in Golden Age Spanish. However, this hypothesis does not support Copple's (2011) findings because she found that the present perfect was favored by atelic verbs (activities and states) in Medieval Spanish and Modern Spanish. This discrepancy is due to the coding criteria; recall that Copple included all occurrences of the present perfect, which contained perfect usages. Consequently, the present perfect was favored by atelic verbs because continuative perfects are compatible with atelic verbs (Schwenter & Torres Cacoullos, 2008).

(5.8) a. Iguales las tuviera el desdichado que **ha muerto**, según dicen, a Reynero, y le van a buscar por todo el mundo. (Los Locos de Valencia)
The same would have the wretched that died, or so they say, Reynero, and they are going to look for him everywhere.

b. Mire señor, que aquellos son frailes de San Benito, y el coche debe de ser de alguna gente pasajera: mire que digo que mire bien lo que hace, no sea el diablo que le engañe. Ya te **he dicho**, Sancho, respondió Don Quijote, que sabes poco de achaques de aventuras: lo que yo digo es verdad, y ahora lo verás. (El Quijote)

Look sire, those are frails of Saint Benito, and the carriage
should be of some passing people: look I am telling you
to think carefully what you are doing, it could be the devil
fooling you. I already told you, Sancho, replied Don Quijote,
you know little of the adventure's aliments: What I say is the
truth, and now you will see it.

The distribution of the present perfect was analyzed according to grammatical person, as illustrated in Table 5.16. It can be observed that the present perfect was used more frequently with third person subjects in the three periods. Example (5.9a) shows an example of the present perfect with a third person subject. Additionally, the present perfect was used frequently with first person subjects in Golden Age Spanish and Modern Spanish. Example (5.9b) demonstrates a use of the present perfect with a first person subject. These results partially support Schwenter and Torres Cacoullos' (2008) hypothesis, which states that the present perfect is subjective and would be used more frequently with first person subjects, because it was used more frequently with third person subjects followed by first person subjects.

(5.9) a. Ya estamos aquí…aquí le traigo a su primo. —Nos *ha visto*—dijo el caballero, estirando el pescuezo hasta el último grado—. (Doña Perfecta)
We are already here…I bring your cousin. —She saw us— said the gentleman, stretching his neck as much as he could—.
   b. –Yo *he hecho* muy mal–se decía–en predicar allí debí haberme callado. (Pepita Jiménez)
–I have done very badly–she said to herself– preaching there I should have shut up.

Table 5.16 Distribution of the present perfect across centuries according to grammatical person

	First person	Second person	Third person	Total
Medieval Spanish	1 (20%)	1 (20%)	3 (60%)	5 (100%)
Golden Age Spanish	10 (19.6%)	9 (17.6%)	32 (62.7%)	51 (100%)
Modern Spanish	12 (46.2%)	1 (3.8%)	13 (50%)	26 (100%)

5.5 Progressive constructions

This section presents the results regarding the progressive constructions. Table 5.17 illustrates the different progressive constructions found in the data. It can be observed that the progressive constructions have an overall low frequency of use, which did not allow to perform statistical analyses. Additionally, the frequency of the progressive constructions increased from Medieval Spanish to Golden Age Spanish. However, their frequency decreased from Golden Age Spanish to Modern Spanish. Finally, it is worth highlighting the overall low frequency of the preterit progressive with *estar*.

Since statistical analyses could not be performed, this section explores trends found in the data. First, the aspectual function of the imperfect and preterit progressives with *estar* are examined (Tables 5.18 and 5.19). The progressive constructions with *estar* were mainly used to express a progressive aspectual function, as illustrated in example (5.10). These results confirm previous accounts on the imperfect progressive with *estar* since they stated that this form is used to express progressive aspectual function (Chaston, 1991; Delgado-Díaz, in press; King & Suñer, 1980; Lamanna, 2008, 2012; Quesada, 1993; Solé & Solé, 1976; Westfall, 1995). On the contrary, this finding does not support previous investigations regarding the preterit progressive. Previous studies attribute a progressive and perfective aspectual function to the preterit progressive (Comrie, 1976; Solé & Solé, 1976; Westfall, 1995, 2003). However, the present data suggests that it is mainly used to express a progressive function. This finding resonates with Delgado-Díaz' (in press) results which found that the preterit progressive with *estar* is mainly used to express a progressive function.

Table 5.17 Distribution of the progressive constructions across centuries

	Medieval Spanish	Golden Age Spanish	Modern Spanish	Total
Imperfect progressive with *estar*	28 (31.8%)	44 (50%)	16 (18.2%)	88 (100%)
Imperfect progressive with other auxiliary verbs	16 (38.1%)	16 (38.1%)	10 (23.8%)	42 (100%)
Preterit progressive with *estar*	1 (5.9%)	13 (76.4%)	3 (17.7%)	17 (100%)
Preterit progressive with other auxiliary verbs	12 (46.2%)	9 (34.6%)	5 (19.2)	26 (100%)

Table 5.18 Distribution of the imperfect progressive with *estar* across centuries

	Habitual	Progressive	Perfective	Indeterminate	Total
Medieval Spanish	0	19 (67.9%)	0	9 (32.1%)	28 (100%)
Golden Age Spanish	0	36 (81.8%)	0	8 (17.2%)	44 (100%)
Modern Spanish	0	13 (81.3%)	0	3 (18.8%)	16 (100%)

Table 5.19 Distribution of the preterit progressive with *estar* across centuries

	Habitual	Progressive	Perfective	Indeterminate	Total
Medieval Spanish	0	1 (100%)	0	0	1 (100%)
Golden Age Spanish	0	9 (69.2%)	0	4 (30.8%)	13 (100%)
Modern Spanish	0	2 (66.7%)	0	1 (33.3%)	3 (100%)

(5.10) Todos los que eran en la hueste e en la çibdat ***estavan parando*** mientes a lo que fazían estos cavalleros e maravillávanse mucho en que se detenían; pero que les semejava que estavan razonando... (Caballero de Zifar)
All that were in the company and in the city were stopping because of what these knights were doing and they were amazed that they were stopping; but they thought they were reasoning...

Tables 5.18 and 5.19 show that the imperfect and preterit progressives with *estar* were used to express indeterminate aspectual functions. The fragment in (5.11) illustrates a use of the preterit progressive with *estar* in an indeterminate aspectual context. This case was coded as indeterminate because the context does not provide sufficient cues to determine if it is progressive or perfective.

(5.11) Y confirmo ésto, por haber visto que cuando ***estuve*** por las bardas del corral ***mirando*** los actos de tu triste tragedia, no me fue posible subir por ellas, ni menos pude apearme de Rocinante... (El Quijote)

And he confirmed this, by having seen when I was on top of the corral watching the act of your sad tragedy, it was not possible to go up, nor could I get off Rocinante...

The progressive constructions with *estar* are examined according to locative co-occurrence, adjacency, association, and fusion. Recall that these variables are supposed to track the grammaticalization degree of progressive constructions (Bybee & Torres Cacoullos, 2009). Table 5.20 illustrates the distribution of the imperfect and preterit progressives with *estar*. Locative co-occurrence indicates the number of cases that appeared with a locative construction; adjacency indicates the number of cases that appeared without intervening material; association shows the cases that appeared with one -ndo form associated to an auxiliary verb; and fusion indicates the cases in which the clitic was placed in front of the auxiliary verb. Regarding the imperfect progressive with *estar*, the results indicate that rate in which it co-occurred with locative expressions decreased over time. The cases without intervening material decreased form Medieval Spanish to Golden Age Spanish, but it increased in Modern Spanish. Additionally, the number of cases of one -ndo form associated with one auxiliary verb decreased from Medieval Spanish to Golden Age Spanish, but it decreased to Modern Spanish. Regarding fusion, recall that Bybee and Torres Cacoullos (2009) stated that the clitic is place in front of the auxiliary verbs in highly grammaticalized constructions. However, there were few uses of clitics in the data to clearly establish a pattern. The fragment in (5.12) illustrates an imperfect progressive with *estar* without a locative expression, intervening material, with one -ndo form associated to the auxiliary verb, and a clitic placed in front of auxiliary verb.

Table 5.20 Progressive constructions distribution of the progressive constructions regarding locative co-occurrence, adjacency, association, and fusion

Factor	Imperfect progressive with estar			Preterit progressive with estar		
	Medieval Spanish	*Golden Age Spanish*	*Modern Spanish*	*Medieval Spanish*	*Golden Age Spanish*	*Modern Spanish*
Locative co-occurrence	17 (60.7%)	14 (31.8%)	5 (31.3%)	0	4 (30.8%)	0
Adjacency	16 (57.1%)	30 (68.2%)	9 (56.3%)	0	8 (61.5%)	3 (100%)
Association	23 (82.1%)	30 (68.2%)	12 (75%)	1 (100%)	11 (84.6%)	3 (100%)
Fusion	1 (3.6%)	8 (18.2%)	1 (6.3%)	0	4 (30.8%)	0

(5.12) Ahora le *estaba diciendo* a Rosario que esta ciudad y esta casa me son tan agradables, que me gustaría vivir y morir aquí. (Doña Perfecta)
Just now I was telling Rosarito that this city and this house are so pleasing to me that I would like to live and die here.

With respect to the preterit progressive, Table 5.20 shows that the only case found in Medieval Spanish did not co-occur with locative expression; it had one -ndo form associated to the auxiliary verb, and it had intervening material between the auxiliary verb and the -ndo form, as illustrated in example (5.13a). In Golden Age Spanish, the preterit progressive with *estar* was used four times with locative expressions, eight times without intervening material, 11 times with one -ndo form associated with an auxiliary verb, and four times with the clitic in front of the auxiliary verb. Finally, in Modern Spanish three cases were found, which were used without locative expressions, without intervening material, and with one -ndo form associated to an auxiliary verb. There was only one case with a clitic which was attached to the -ndo form. The fragment in (5.13b) illustrates a use of the preterit progressive with *estar* without locative expressions, without intervening material, with one -ndo form associated to the auxiliary verb, and the clitic attached to the -ndo form.

(5.13) a. ...luego fue levantada e enbió por la muger del Cavallero Zifar, e sienpre *estovieron* en oraçión, *rogando* a Dios que guardase los suyos de mal... (Caballero de Zifar)
...then she was woken up and she sent for Knight Zifar's wife, and they were always in prayer, asking God to protect their men from harm...

b. Aun así, gracias a la tardanza del galán, la pobre Pepita *estuvo deshaciéndose*, llena de ansiedad y de angustia, desde que terminó sus oraciones y súplicas con el Niño Jesús hasta que vio dentro del despacho al otro niño. (Pepita Jiménez)
Even though, thanks to the handsome man's delay, poor Pepita was undoing herself, full of anxiety and anguish, since she finished her prayers and pleads to Baby Jesus until she saw the other boy in the study.

Table 5.20 suggests that, even though both constructions demonstrated more or less the same tendencies, the imperfect progressive with *estar* is in a more advanced grammaticalization stage than the

106 Results

Table 5.21 Distribution of the imperfect progressive with other auxiliary verbs across centuries

	Medieval Spanish	Golden Age Spanish	Modern Spanish
Auxiliary verb			
Andar 'to walk'	6 (37.4%)	3 (18.8%)	0
Ir 'to go'	9 (56.3%)	11 (68.8%)	4 (40%)
Seguir 'to keep doing'	0	0	4 (40%)
Pasar 'to spend time doing'	0	1 (6.2%)	0
Volver 'to come back'	0	1 (6.2%)	0
Venir 'to come'	1 (6.3%)	0	2 (20%)
Total	16 (100%)	16 (100%)	10 (100%)

preterit progressive with *estar*. This hypothesis is based on the low frequency of use of the preterit progressive with *estar*. Consequently, this would imply that the imperfect progressive with *estar* grammaticalized before the preterit progressive with *estar*. Additionally, these results suggest that fusion may not correlate with the degree of grammaticalization of these past progressive constructions because many cases appeared without any clitic.

The analysis yielded cases of progressive constructions with other auxiliary verbs. Table 5.21 illustrates the different auxiliary verbs used with the imperfect progressive across time. It can be observed that *andar* 'to walk' was used in the three periods (5.14a). Other auxiliary verbs were found in specific periods; for instance, *ir* 'to go' (5.14b) was the most frequent auxiliary verb in Medieval Spanish and Golden Age Spanish, but it was not found in Modern Spanish. *Seguir* 'to keep doing' (5.14c) was found in Modern Spanish, while *pasar* 'to spend time doing' (5.14d) and *volver* 'to come back' (5.14d) were found in Golden Age Spanish. Finally, *venir* 'to come' (5.14e) was found in Medieval Spanish and Golden Age Spanish.

(5.14) a. …la señora de la villa quando oyó este ruido e tan grant llanto que fazían, maravillose qué podría ser, e **andava demandando** quel dixiesen que qué era. (Caballero de Zifar)
…when the lady of the town heard that noise and that great cry that they were making, she wondered what it could be, and was asking around so that someone would tell her what it was.

b. Pero él iba tan puesto en que eran gigantes, que ni oía las voces de su escudero Sancho, ni echaba de ver, aunque estaba ya bien cerca, lo que eran; antes *iba diciendo* en voces altas: non fuyades, cobardes y viles criaturas, que un solo caballero es el que os acomete. (El Quijote)
But he was so sure that those were giants, that he did not even hear his squire Sancho's voice, nor did he even take a look to see what they were, even though he was already near; before he was saying in a loud voice: do not flee, coward and vile creatures, that it is only one knight charges you.

c. Ya hemos visto por las cartas la vehemencia de su pasión; pero él *seguía enfrenándola* con los mismos afectos piadosos y consideraciones elevadas de que en las cartas da larga muestra, y que podemos omitir aquí para no pecar de prolijos. (Pepita Jiménez)
We have already seen in the letters the vehemence of his passion; but he kept dominating her with the same merciful affections and high considerations of which he shows in his letters, that we can omit here so as not to be verbose.

d. En resolución, él se enfrascó tanto en su lectura, que se le *pasaban* las noches *leyendo* de claro en claro.
(El Quijote)
In conclusion, he immersed himself so much in his reading, that he would spend nights on end reading from dusk until dawn.

e. Luego *volvía diciendo*, como si verdaderamente fuera enamorado: "¡Oh, princesa Dulcinea, señora de este cautivo corazón!" (El Quijote)
Then he would return saying, as if he was truly in love: "Oh, princess Dulcinea, lady of this captive heart!"

f. E a las bozes que dava el otro fijuelo que *venía fuyendo*, bolvió la cabeça la dueña e vio cómo la leona levava el un fijuelo, e començó a dar bozes. (Caballero de Zifar)
And the screams that the other child was doing that he was fleeing, the lady turned her head and saw the lion taking one of her children away, and she started to scream.

Regarding the aspectual function of the imperfect progressive with other auxiliary verbs, it was found that it was mainly used to express a progressive aspectual function (14 cases [87.5%] in Medieval Spanish,

12 cases [75%] in Golden Age Spanish, and ten cases [100%] in Modern Spanish). Example (5.15a) illustrates a case of the imperfect progressive with *ir* 'to go' with a progressive function. Additionally, there were few cases of this construction with an indeterminate aspectual function (two cases [12.5%] in Medieval Spanish and four cases [25%] in Golden Age Spanish). The fragment in (5.15b) illustrates a use of this construction with an indeterminate aspectual function. *Iva aviendo* 'were having' was coded as indeterminate because the context does not provide sufficient information to determine if it is progressive or habitual.

(5.15)   a.   Con esta licencia se acomodó Sancho lo mejor que pudo sobre su jumento, y sacando de las alforjas lo que en ellas había puesto, **iba caminando** y **comiendo** detrás de su amo muy despacio… (El Quijote)
With this license Sancho settled in the best he could in his donkey, and taking out what he had put in the saddlebag, he was riding and eating behind his master very slowly.

   b.   Aguijava el conde e pensava de andar, tornando va la cabeça e catándos' atrás,
miedo **iva aviendo** que mio Cid se repintrá,
lo que non ferié el caboso
por cuanto en el mundo ha… (El Cantar del Mio Cid)
The count spurred and thought about going,
He turned his head and looked at them,
They were having fear that mio Cid would regret
That which the captain did not announce
To everyone in the world…

There were also cases of the preterit progressive with other auxiliary verbs, as illustrated in Table 5.22. This table shows that *andar* 'to walk' (5.16a) was used in the three time periods. On the contrary, the other auxiliary verbs were not documented in these time periods. For example, *ir* 'to go' (5.16b) was found in Medieval Spanish and Golden Age Spanish. *Seguir* 'to keep doing' (5.16c) was used in Golden Age Spanish and Modern Spanish. *Continuar* 'to continue' (5.16d) and *quedar* 'to remain' (5.16e) were found in Modern Spanish.

(5.16)   a.   …santa Susaña del falso criminal;
por tierra **andidiste** treínta e dos años, Señor spirital,
mostrando los miráculos, por én avemos qué fablar…
(El Cantar del Mio Cid)

...saint Susaña of the false criminal; You walked the earth
for thirty two years, spiritual Lord,
Showing the miracles, because of that we have to talk

b. ...dándole una lanzada en el aspa, la volvió el viento con tanta furia, que hizo la lanza pedazos, llevándose tras sí al caballo y al caballero, que *fue rodando* muy maltrecho por el campo. (El Quijote)
...hitting the blade with the spear, the wind turned it with such fury, that it destroyed the lance, taking the horse and the knight with it, that he rolled battered through the meadow.

c. Durante mucho tiempo doña Perfecta *siguió viviendo* en Orbajosa. (Doña Perfecta)
For a long time Doña Perfecta continued living in Orbajosa.

d. Luego que los cuatro se reunieron, *continuaron paseando*. (Doña Perfecta)
After the four of them got together, they continue strolling.

e. ...casi todos los viajeros de segunda y tercera clase se *quedaron durmiendo* o *bostezando* dentro de los coches, porque el frío penetrante de la madrugada no convidaba a pasear por el desamparado andén. (Doña Perfecta)
...almost all the second and third class passengers stayed sleeping or yawning inside the carts, because the penetrating morning cold did not invite to stroll along the lonely platform.

Table 5.22 Distribution of the preterit progressive with other auxiliary verbs across centuries

	Medieval Spanish	Golden Age Spanish	Modern Spanish
Auxiliary verb			
Andar 'to walk'	2 (16.7%)	1 (8.3%)	0
Ir 'to go'	10 (83.3%)	6 (50%)	1 (12.5%)
Seguir 'to keep doing'	0	1 (8.3%)	1 (12.5%)
Continuar 'to continue'	0	0	1 (12.5%)
Quedar 'to remain'	0	0	2 (25%)
Total	12 (100%)	8 (100%)	5 (100%)

Regarding the aspectual function of the preterit progressive with other auxiliary verbs, the results indicate that it was mainly used to express a progressive function (three cases [25%] in Medieval Spanish, eight cases [100%] in Golden Age Spanish, and four cases [80%] in Modern Spanish). The fragment in (5.17a) illustrates a use of the preterit progressive with other auxiliary verbs expressing a progressive aspectual function, in which Don Quijote rolled for a while through the meadow. There were cases coded as indeterminate in Medieval Spanish (nine cases [75%]) and in Modern Spanish (one case [20%]). The preterit progressive with *andar* 'to walk' in (5.17b) was coded as indeterminate because the context does not allow to determine if the event is progressive or habitual.

(5.17) a. Cayó Rocinante, y *fue rodando* su amo una buena pieza por el campo, y queriéndose levantar, jamás pudo. (El Quijote)
Rocinante fell, and her master rolled a good distance through the meadow, and wanting to get up, he never managed.

b. E cuidaron quel matador que era salido por aquella puerta, e *andudieron buscando* e non fallaron rastro dél. (Caballero de Zifar)
And they knew that the murderer exited through that door, and they walked around looking and they did not find any trace of him.

The results of the progressive constructions with other auxiliary verbs reveal that the most frequent auxiliary verbs were movement verbs. In fact, *andar* 'to walk' and *ir* 'to go' were the most frequent auxiliary verbs with the imperfect and preterit progressives. Torres Cacoullos (2000) found a high frequency of *ir* 'to go' and *andar* 'to walk' in 16th century and early 19th century Spanish. However, Torres Cacoullos noted that the frequency of *ir* 'to go' declined while the frequency of *estar* increased. Bybee et al. (1994) found that progressive constructions in most of the languages in their study had locative sources. This could imply that Spanish shifted from a movement source to a locative one. The present data found a similar trend since the frequency of use of movement auxiliary verbs, specially *andar* 'to go', declined through time. However, the results did not reveal a striking rise of *estar*; on the contrary, there was a decrease of past progressive constructions with *estar* in Modern Spanish. This is possible that the progressive constructions are not associated with written texts (Torres Cacoullos,

2000). For instance, Torres Cacoullos (2000) found that the present progressive had a relative frequency of 5.1% in early 20th century prose. On the contrary, this construction had a relative frequency of 19.7% in Mexican Popular speech.

It is worth noticing that the past progressive constructions with *estar* have a lower overall frequency than the present progressive in Modern Spanish (1.7% with the imperfect progressive, .8% with the preterit progressive in contrast to 5.1% present progressive). This finding may suggest that past progressive constructions with *estar* grammaticalize later than the present progressive (Delgado-Díaz, 2018a, Torres Cacoullos, personal communication). The next chapter explores the implications of the results discussed.

6 Discussion and conclusions

6.1 Introduction

The discussion in this chapter is guided by the research questions, which are:

1. What are the patterns of variation found in the past-time expression in Spanish?
   What is the distribution of the imperfect, preterit, present perfect, imperfect progressive, and preterit progressive in Spanish diachronic data? Which forms have overlapping functions?
2. How does Grammaticalization Theory explain these patterns of variability?
   Do the linguistic factors that predict the use of different past forms change through time?

Additionally, this chapter discusses other findings related to Grammaticalization Theory that fall outside the research questions.

6.2 Patterns of variation

This section discusses the results pertaining to the first research question, which inquiries about the distribution and possible overlapping functions of the different past aspectual forms. The results indicate that the preterit and imperfect were the most frequent forms. More specifically, there were 1,068 cases of the preterit in Medieval Spanish, 1,025 cases in Golden Age Spanish, and 1,011 cases in Modern Spanish. There were 420 cases of the imperfect in Medieval Spanish, 641 cases in Golden Age Spanish, and 858 cases in Modern Spanish. Other past forms had low frequencies of use; for example, there were five cases of the present perfect in Medieval Spanish, 51 cases in Golden Age

Spanish, and 26 cases in Modern Spanish[1]. There were 26 cases of the imperfect progressive with *estar* in Medieval Spanish, 44 cases in Golden Age Spanish, and 16 cases in Modern Spanish. The analysis yielded one case of the preterit progressive with *estar* in Medieval Spanish, .13 cases in Golden Age Spanish, and three cases in Modern Spanish. Additionally, there were other progressive constructions with different auxiliary verbs. There were 16 cases of the imperfect progressive with other auxiliary verbs in Medieval Spanish, 16 cases in Golden Age Spanish, and ten cases in Modern Spanish. The analysis found 12 cases of the preterit progressive with other auxiliary verbs in Medieval Spanish, nine cases in Golden Age Spanish, and five cases in Modern Spanish.

The aspectual function of each form was analyzed to determine overlapping uses. It was found that the imperfect was mainly used to express habitual and progressive functions across centuries, which confirms previous research (Ayres, 2009; Baker & Quesda, 2011; Bello, 1847; Bybee et al., 1994; Cipria & Roberts, 2000; Comrie, 1976; Delgado-Díaz, in press; Lamanna, 2008, 2012; Montrul & Slabakova, 2003; RAE, 1973, 2010; Rodríguez-Ramalle, 2005). This finding suggests that the prototypical meaning of the imperfect is progressiveness and habituality. However, there were limited cases of the imperfect expressing perfectivity with a rate of 9.8% in Medieval Spanish, 1.7% in Golden Age Spanish, and 3.3% in Modern Spanish. This finding supports previous investigations which documented perfective uses of the imperfect (Ayres, 2009; Delgado-Díaz, in press; Doiz, 2011; Rodriguez, 2004; Silva-Corvalán, 1994; Zentella, 1997). More specifically, this finding resonates with Delgado-Díaz (in press), who found a similar distribution in Puerto Rican Spanish. Furthermore, the use of the imperfect in perfective contexts is not due to contact with English, as proposed by Silva-Corvalán (1994) and Zentella (1997), since this phenomenon can be traced from Medieval Spanish.

Regarding the preterit, this form was used more frequently with a perfective aspectual function in the three periods analyzed, suggesting that it is its main function. This finding supports previous claims on the preterit (Alcina Franch & Blecua, 1975; Bello, 1847; Delgado-Díaz, in press; RAE, 1973, 2010; Serrano, 2006; Westfall, 1995, 2003). However, there were limited cases in which the preterit was used to express habitual and progressive functions. The analysis revealed that the preterit was used to express a progressive function 2.5% of the time in Medieval Spanish, 1.7% in Golden Age Spanish, and 2.4% in Modern Spanish. This finding supports previous investigations in which it has been documented that the preterit can express progressive events (Ayres, 2009; Brucart, 2003;

114 Discussion and conclusions

Champion, 1973; Delgado-Díaz, in press). Additionally, the preterit was used to convey a habitual meaning .2% of the time in Medieval Spanish, .3% in Golden Age Spanish, and .1% in Modern Spanish. These results suggest that the preterit is more compatible with progressive events than with habitual ones, which implies that variation between the preterit and imperfect is more likely to occur within the progressive domain. Delgado-Díaz (in press) found similar results in Puerto Rican Spanish. This scholar found that the preterit's main function is perfective and that it was used more frequently to express a progressive function than a habitual one.

The variable patterns described for the preterit represent a stable variation. Figure 6.1 illustrates that the use of this form with progressive and habitual aspectual functions does not fluctuate much across centuries. Tagliamonte (2012) argued that a flat pattern corresponds to a stable linguistic variable (p.55). The imperfect shows a slightly different pattern; Figure 6.1 shows that the frequency of use of the imperfect in perfective contexts lowered from Medieval Spanish to Golden Age Spanish, but it stabilizes in Golden Age Spanish and Modern Spanish. Consequently, this graph suggests that the preterit and imperfect are not undergoing language change regarding their aspectual function; rather, the results show patterns of stable variation.

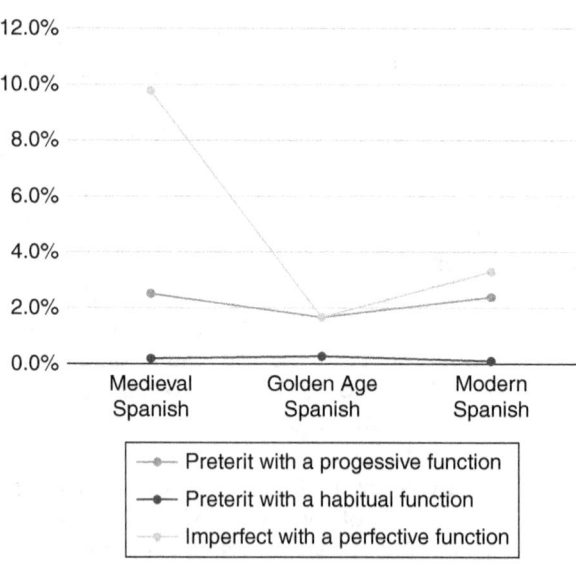

Figure 6.1 Distribution of the preterit in progressive and habitual functions and the imperfect with a perfective function

Discussion and conclusions 115

With respect to the present perfect with a perfective aspectual function, the results found an increase from Medieval Spanish to Golden Age Spanish (five cases to 51 cases), followed by a slight decrease from Golden Age Spanish to Modern Spanish (51 cases to 26). This distribution may suggest that the present perfect grammaticalized further to a perfective function, expanding its contexts of use from Medieval Spanish to Golden Age Spanish. The low frequency of use in Modern Spanish may be due to the type of literary works analyzed, which did not produce favorable contexts for the present perfect with a perfective function. The results suggest that this construction with a perfective function is used frequently in conversations, as included in *Los Locos de Valencia*.

It is important to notice the sharp contrast between the present study and Copple's (2011) investigation. Recall that Copple (2011) investigated the perfect-to-perfective grammaticalization of the present perfect from a diachronic perspective. The differences between these investigations are due to the coding method employed. Copple (2011) coded for every instance of this form while the present research only included those items which express a perfective function. Variationist analysis on the present perfect tend to include every instance of this construction (see the discussion in chapter 3). However, recall that including all the uses of the present perfect in the analysis may not be the best manner to study its perfect-to-perfective grammaticalization. This type of analysis includes variable (perfective uses of the present perfect) and non-variable (perfect uses of the present perfect) contexts. Consequently, the results of these investigations may not present the factors that favor the use of this construction with perfective function. Delgado-Díaz (2018a) recommends using aspectual function as the dependent variable, which should determine the factors that favor the use of the present perfect with a perfective function.

Regarding the imperfect progressive with *estar*, this construction was used to express progressive events in the three periods analyzed. This finding supports previous investigations which argue that the imperfect progressive is used to convey a progressive function (Delgado-Díaz, in press; King & Suñer, 1980; Lamanna, 2008, 2012; Quesada, 1993; Solé & Solé, 1976; Westfall, 1995). It is worth mentioning that the imperfect progressive was not used to express a habitual aspectual function, as documented in contemporary Spanish (Chaston, 1991; Delgado-Díaz, in press; Lamanna, 2008, 2012). This finding suggests that this construction had not grammaticalized a habitual function by Modern Spanish. Similar results were found for the imperfect progressive with other auxiliary verbs since it was mainly used to express a progressive function in

116 Discussion and conclusions

all three time periods. This may imply that imperfect progressive with other auxiliary verbs fulfil a similar function as the imperfect progressive with *estar* (i.e., layering). Torres Cacoullos (2000) explained that there are older auxiliary verbs (i.e., *ir* 'to go' and *andar* 'to walk') coexisting with newer ones (i.e., *estar*). Recall that during grammaticalization several grams can coexist and express similar functions (Bybee et al., 1994; Heine, 2003). This may explain why these different auxiliary verbs have similar functions.

The preterit progressive with *estar* and the preterit progressive with other auxiliary verbs were mainly used to express a progressive meaning in the time periods analyzed. This finding does not seem to support previous investigations which attribute a dual progressive and perfective aspectual function (Comrie, 1976; Solé & Solé, 1976; Westfall 1995, 2003). In addition, this construction was not used to express a habitual function, as documented by Delgado-Díaz (in press). This could imply that the preterit progressive had not developed this function by the 19th century. However, further research is required in this regard because of the low frequency of the preterit progressive in the corpus.

This review allows for a determination of which forms have overlapping functions. First, it is important to review the aspectual system according to previous investigations. It can be seen in Figure 6.2 that the preterit, imperfect, and preterit progressive can be used to express perfective, progressive, and habitual functions. The imperfect progressive

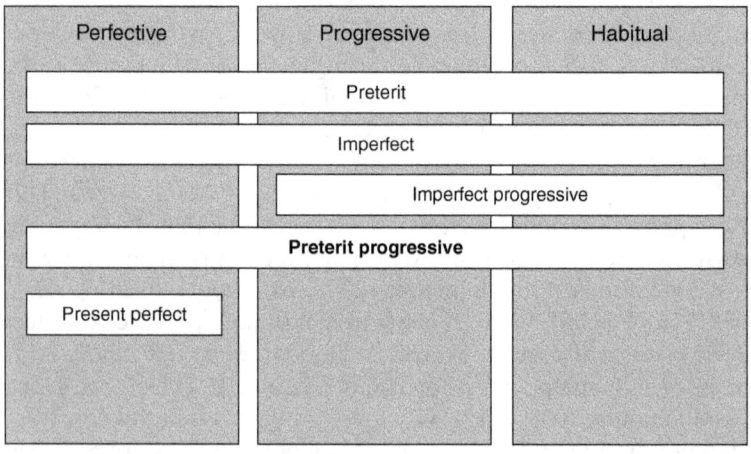

Figure 6.2 Representation of the aspectual functions of each form according to previous investigations

Discussion and conclusions 117

can be used to convey progressiveness and habituality and the present perfect can express perfective events.

On the contrary, Figure 6.3 illustrates the aspectual function of each form based on the results of the present investigation. This figure illustrates each aspectual domain, perfective, progressive, and habitual, in dark gray areas. The black areas between each function represent indeterminate contexts. The solid color of the bands is associated with prototypical meanings. Consequently, if a form has a solid gray over the perfective domain, it means that it is part of its prototypical meaning. On the contrary, a diffused or translucid color means that a form can express the aspectual function or functions that the band covers, but it is not associated with a prototypical meaning. For example, if a band covers progressive and habitual domains with a translucid shade, it means that this form can express habitual and progressive meaning, but these meanings are not part of its prototypical meaning. Consequently, it can be noted that the preterit's prototypical function is perfectivity; this can be seen in the solid gray color of the preterit in the perfective area (see solid gray band in the figure). This figure also shows that there are limited contexts in which the preterit can express a progressive and habitual function. This is represented in the diffused gray of the preterit that covers progressive and habitual aspectual functions. The imperfect is used prototypically to convey progressive and habitual functions. Additionally, there are limited contexts in which it can express a perfective function. The progressive constructions are mainly

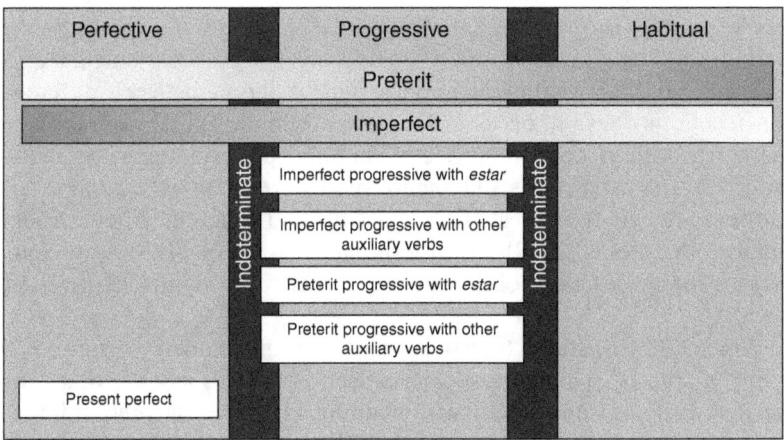

Figure 6.3 Representation of the aspectual function according to each construction

used to express a progressive function. These forms are represented in the progressive domain with a solid gray color since they were used primarily to express a progressive function. Additionally, it can be noted that these forms overextend the progressive domain but do not reach the perfective or habitual domains causing indeterminate contexts. Finally, the present perfect is represented in the perfective area with a solid gray color.

Regarding overlapping uses, Figure 6.3 shows that the preterit and imperfect share some contexts of use, although limited. This suggests that the imperfect prototypical functions are habitual and progressive, while the preterit's prototypical function is perfective. Recall that the variation of the preterit and imperfect is stable, which suggests that the imperfect is not moving to semantic areas of the preterit and vice versa. Additionally, it was found that the preterit and present perfect interact within the perfective domain. Furthermore, this analysis revealed that most of these forms compete within the progressive aspectual domain. That is, the imperfect and the past progressive constructions share progressiveness as part of their prototypical meaning, which may cause instances of layering (i.e., two or more constructions expressing similar grammatical functions). Furthermore, this figure illustrates that investigating forms with a dichotomous perspective (i.e., preterit vs imperfect, preterit vs present perfect, etc.) does not account for how these forms interact with each other. Therefore, tense and aspect variationist analyses should circumscribe the envelope of variation within aspectual domains (Delgado-Díaz, 2018a, in press).

Figure 6.3 highlights another issue regarding the form-function symmetry assumption. Recall that Poplack (2018) rejects this assumption stating that language variation is full of neutralized contexts and asymmetries. This statement implies that variation between different constructions does not necessarily express different functions (i.e., they share neutralized contexts). Recall that the preterit, imperfect, past progressive constructions may share neutralized contexts because all of them are able to express the same aspectual function. These results support Poplack's (2018) hypothesis since Spanish past expressions present many instances of form-function asymmetry and neutralized contexts.

Poplack (2018) stated that the form-function symmetry assumption is at the core of sociolinguistics because researchers assume that syntactic variation entails a change of meaning. However, the present investigation provides evidence which indicates that this problem extends to other areas of linguistic research. This issue can be observed in grammarian analyses, generative literature, second language acquisition studies, variationist studies, among others. Consequently, it is argued that Poplack's (2018) recommendation of sociolinguists abandoning the form-function asymmetry assumption should be applied to other linguistic areas of research. This is especially important to grammaticalization investigations since grammaticalizing constructions may present cases of form-function asymmetry and neutralized contexts.

6.3 Grammaticalization Theory and language change

This section addresses the second research question which inquires if Grammaticalization Theory can explain the patterns of variability found and if the factors that influence past-time expressions changed through time. It is worth highlighting that statistical analyses could only be performed on the preterit and imperfect. There were not sufficient cases of other past-time expressions to perform statistical analyses. Consequently, this section reviews the significant factors of the preterit and imperfect and trends found in the data for other past forms.

Regarding the preterit and imperfect, Tables 6.1 and 6.2 illustrate their constraint hierarchy in each period. It can be observed that aspectual function was the most important factor for both forms across centuries. However, some factors weakened while others strengthened over time. Additionally, it can be noted that some factors become significant while others lose their significance. These findings indicate that the preterit and imperfect have undergone grammaticalization processes since change of linguistic constraints through time may indicate grammaticalization processes (Torres Cacoullos, 2012). It is possible that these changes are caused by the emergence of the past progressives, which may have caused the Spanish aspectual system to shift since much of these forms overlap in the progressive domain.

In addition, these findings may explain why grammar analysis varies diachronically with respect to different linguistic factors that influence the choice between the preterit and imperfect, as documented by Delgado-Díaz (2014). Poplack and Dion (2009) investigated different grammar proposals regarding the use of French synthetic future, analytical future, and simple present with a future time reference. Among their results, these scholars found diachronic variation with respect to the different functions attributed to these future expressions. They argue that one possible explanation is that this variability may respond to grammaticalization processes that these constructions experienced. In other words, different grammar analysis emerged as these constructions gained or lost grammatical functions over time. Consequently, the results from the preterit and imperfect seem to confirm that diachronic

120 Discussion and conclusions

Table 6.1 Constraint hierarchy of the imperfect according to period

Medieval Spanish	Golden Age Spanish	Modern Spanish
Aspectual function	Aspectual function	Aspectual function
Type of information	Lexical semantics	Type of information
Priming	Priming	Frame of temporal reference
	Type of information	Priming

Table 6.2 Constraint hierarchy of the preterit according to period

Medieval Spanish	Golden Age Spanish	Modern Spanish
Aspectual function	Aspectual function	Aspectual function
Type of information	Grammatical person	Type of information
Priming	Specificity of the subject	

evolution in grammar analysis corresponds to grammaticalization processes (Delgado-Díaz, 2014; Poplack & Dion, 2009).

Now then, when comparing the significant factors of the imperfect with those of the preterit, it can be noticed that these forms share the same predictors in Medieval Spanish. On the contrary, these two forms have different predictors in Golden Age Spanish and Modern Spanish, except for aspectual function. This finding has several implications: first, the preterit and imperfect are not as stable as previously thought since their predictors and constraint hierarchy changed through time. Second, the preterit and imperfect are not complete opposites; that is, the preterit is not necessarily used in contrast to the imperfect and vice versa. On the contrary, these forms express specific semantic meanings and nuances that the other does not express.

Regarding the present perfect, the results suggest that lexical semantic may have played a role in the perfect-to-perfective grammaticalization of the present perfect. The analysis found that the present perfect with a perfective meaning was used frequently with achievement verbs across centuries. Then, this construction spread to accomplishment verbs in Golden Age Spanish. This trend can also be observed in Modern Spanish, but the present was less frequently with other semantic classes. This finding could imply that the perfect-to-perfective grammaticalization path of the present perfect may also be motivated by achievement and accomplishment verbs, in addition to temporal proximity and indetermination (Hernández, 2004; Schwenter, 1994; Schwenter & Torres Cacoullos, 2008, among others). However, this finding does not support Copple's (2011) results because she found that the present perfect was favored by atelic verbs in 15th and 17th century Spanish. This may be due to different coding criteria, recall that Copple (2011) coded for all instances of the present perfect, which included variable and non-variable contexts. On the contrary, the present research included the present perfect when it was used to express a perfective aspectual function. Consequently, including only the cases of the present perfect with a perfective function provides a clearer picture of its evolution.

The use of the present perfect with a perfective function with achievement and accomplishment verbs allows the proposition of the following hypothesis: The present perfect with accomplishment and achievement verbs was reanalyzed as perfective by an analogy with the preterit, which is used prototypically with these types of verbs. This hypothesis is presented in Figure 6.4. This figure illustrates that the preterit with achievement and accomplishment verbs is at the center of the perfective aspectual domain because these are the prototypical uses of the preterit. The preterit with other semantic classes is near the center, whereas the present perfect with achievement and accomplishment verbs is represented in the periphery. However, more studies are needed

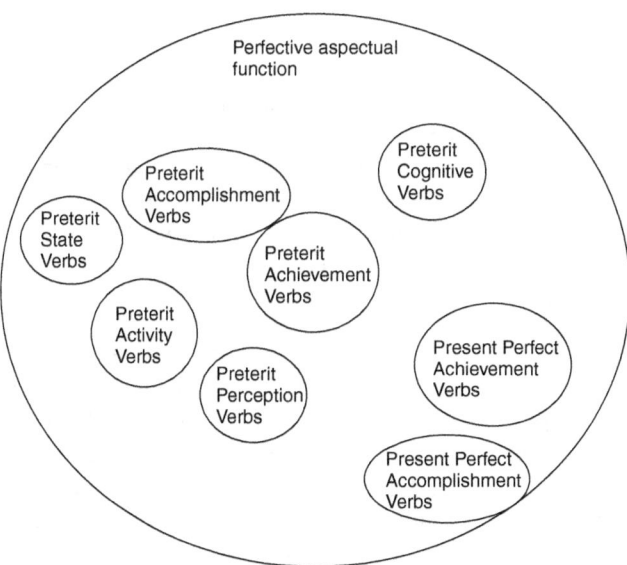

Figure 6.4 Representation of the perfective aspectual function exemplar

122 *Discussion and conclusions*

to confirm this hypothesis due to the small cases of the present perfect with a perfective meaning in the present investigation. Additionally, future studies should investigate how achievement and accomplishment verbs interacts with hodiernal and indeterminate temporal references. Recall that previous studies have found that the perfect-to-perfective grammaticalization occurs through these temporal references (Burgo, 2010; Copple, 2011; Hérnandez, 2004; Howe, 2006; Howe & Schwenter, 2008; Kanwit, Geeslin, & Fafulas, 2015; Schwenter, 1994; Schwenter & Torres Cacoullos, 2008, among others).

The present investigation found few instances of the past progressives: however, some speculations may be drawn with respect to their grammaticalization processes. Before discussing the grammaticalization of the past progressive, it is important to mention some important aspects: first, Grammaticalization Theory predicts that progressive constructions develop later in languages (Bybee et al., 1994). In fact, Penny (2000) mentions that Spanish progressive constructions were not inherited from Latin, which implies that these constructions were developed later in Spanish. Second, past progressives tend to grammaticalize later than present progressives (Torres Cacoullos, personal communication). Finally, Bybee and Torres Cacoullos (2009) argued that the grammaticalization of progressive constructions can be measured by investigating the co-occurrence of locative constructions, the intervening material between the auxiliary verb and the -ndo form (adjacency), the number of -ndo forms associated to one auxiliary verb (association), and the position of the clitic (fusion). According to these scholars, as the progressive constructions grammaticalize, they tend to appear with less locative constructions, less intervening material between the auxiliary verb and the -ndo form, the auxiliary verb is associated with one -ndo form, and the clitic tends to appear before the auxiliary verb. Consequently, it is important to contrast the past progressives with *estar* with the present progressive to track their grammaticalization processes.

Table 6.3 compares the grammaticalization of the present progressive with *estar* (Bybee & Torres Cacoullos, 2009) with the imperfect progressive with *estar* and the preterit progressive with *estar*. It can be noted that across the centuries the present progressive with *estar* appeared less with locative constructions, with less intervening material, one -ndo form is associated with one auxiliary verb, and the clitic tends to appear before the auxiliary verbs. These results indicate that the present progressive with *estar* behaves more as a single unit in Modern Spanish. A similar pattern was found for the imperfect progressive; however, it is worth noticing that this construction seems to

Table 6.3 Comparison between the present progressive with the past progressives

Factor	Present progressive with estar (Bybee & Torres Cacoullos (2009))			Imperfect progressive with estar			Preterit progressive with estar		
	Medieval Spanish	Golden Age Spanish	Modern Spanish	Medieval Spanish	Golden Age Spanish	Modern Spanish	Medieval Spanish	Golden Age Spanish	Modern Spanish
Locative co-occurrence	54 (40%)	51 (24%)	35 (16%)	17 (60.7%)	14 (31.8%)	5 (31.3%)	0	4 (30.8%)	0
Adjacency	67 (50%)	145 (67%)	169 (78%)	16 (57.1%)	30 (68.2%)	9 (56.3%)	0	8 (61.5%)	3 (100%)
Association	115 (86%)	192 (88%)	199 (92%)	23 (82.1%)	30 (68.2%)	12 (75%)	1 (100%)	11 (84.6%)	3 (100%)
Fusion	11 (50%)	61 (82%)	54 (70%)	1 (3.6%)	8 (18.2%)	1 (6.3%)	0	4 (30.8%)	0

124 Discussion and conclusions

fall behind the present progressive with *estar*. For instance, the imperfect progressive with *estar* starts with a rate of 60.7% of co-occurrence with locative constructions while the present progressive with *estar* starts with 40%. In Modern Spanish, the present progressive with *estar* finishes with 16% rate of locative co-occurrence whereas the imperfect progressive with *estar* ends with a rate of 31.3%. However, the imperfect progressive with *estar* showed a different pattern regarding adjacency since the frequency in which it occurred without intervening material decreased from 68.2% in Golden Age Spanish to 56.3% in Modern Spanish. In other words, it was used with more intervening material in Modern Spanish. Regarding the preterit progressive with *estar*, there were limited uses of this construction in the literary works analyzed. This suggests that the preterit progressive with *estar* is even further behind in the grammaticalization cline.

Consequently, this comparison seems to support the hypothesis which states that the past progressives grammaticalize later than the present ones (Torres Cacoullos, personal communication). Additionally, the contrast between the different progressive constructions allowed determining the specific order of grammaticalization. Figure 6.5 illustrates that the present progressive with *estar* is leading the grammaticalization process, followed by the imperfect progressive with *estar*, while the preterit progressive is in last place.

As a matter of fact, it is suggested that the extension of the past progressives with *estar* is an analogy process from the present progressive *estar*, which spread to the imperfect progressive with *estar* and later to the preterit progressive with *estar*. Hopper and Traugott (2003) argued that analogy can involve a generalization of a rule in the sense that a rule may expand its context of use (p.68). Consequently, it is argued that that the progressive construction first emerged in the present to convey actions that are occurring in a location (Bybee et al., 1994; Torres Cacoullos, 2000, 2012, 2015). Then, the progressive construction extended to the past, appearing with the imperfect progressive with *estar* because both progressive constructions express a progressive aspectual function. Finally, the progressive construction became more generalized and extended to other past auxiliary verbs, as the preterit. Figure 6.6 illustrates this hypothesis.

Present progressive with *estar*	< Imperfect progressive with *estar*	< Preterit progressive with *estar*

Figure 6.5 Grammaticalization order of the Spanish progressive forms

Discussion and conclusions 125

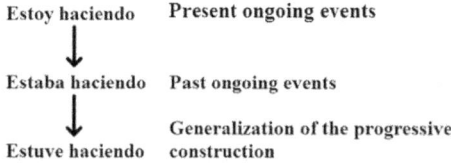

Figure 6.6 Grammaticalization path of the progressive constructions

The present research also found cases of the past progressives with other auxiliary verbs. It was found that *andar* 'to walk' and *ir* 'to go' were the most frequent auxiliary verbs found in the corpus. However, their frequency of use decreased through time, in fact, the analysis did not find cases of *andar* 'to walk' in Modern Spanish. Torres Cacoullos (2000) reported similar findings for the present progressive. This scholar found that the frequency of *andar* 'to go' and *ir* 'to go' decreased while the frequency of *estar* increased. This may suggest that Spanish changed from a movement to a goal progressive source to a locative one. Additionally, this pattern allows us to hypothesize the grammaticalization order of these auxiliary verbs. Their distribution suggests that *andar* 'to walk' is the older auxiliary, followed by *ir* 'to go', while *estar* is the latest auxiliary verb. Figure 6.7 illustrates the distribution of the *andar* 'to walk', *ir* 'to go', and *estar* with both the preterit and imperfect progressives. It can be observed that *andar* 'to walk' and *ir* 'to go' had low frequency of use in Medieval Spanish in comparison with *estar*. This suggests that both *andar* 'to walk' and *ir* 'to go' are in advanced stages in their grammaticalization cline. This hypothesis can be further supported by their steady decline over time. Additionally, this graph suggests that *andar* 'to walk' is closer to the end of its grammaticalization cline in contrast to *ir* 'to go'. The data indicates that *andar* 'to walk' had a lower frequency than *ir* 'to go' and *andar* 'to walk' was not found in Modern Spanish. However, more research is needed to support these hypotheses due to the low frequency of past progressive found in the data.

It is worth highlighting that *estar* did not increase drastically with the past progressives, contrary to the present progressive. In fact, the past progressives increased from Medieval Spanish to Golden Age Spanish, but their frequency decreased in Modern Spanish. This finding suggests that the progressive forms may not be associated with written text. Recall that Torres Cacoullos (2000) documented more cases of the present progressive in oral data than in written documents. Consequently, future research on Spanish progressive construction should include

126 Discussion and conclusions

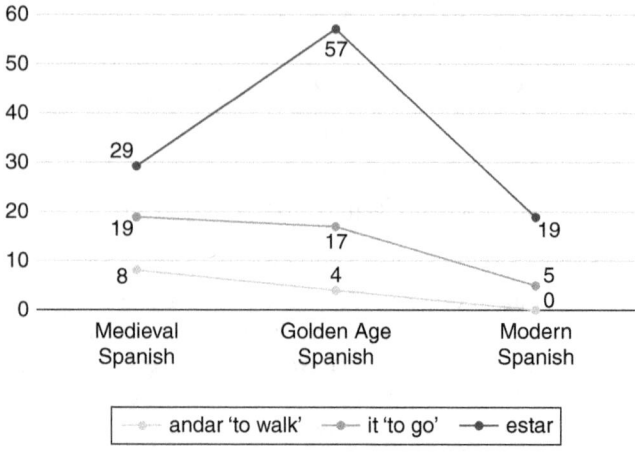

Figure 6.7 Overall distribution of *andar* 'to walk', *ir* 'to go', and *estar*

more plays because they incorporate dialogs and may provide more uses of these constructions.

6.4 Conclusions

This study investigated the historical evolution of different past aspectual forms (i.e., the preterit, imperfect, present perfect, imperfect progressive with *estar*, preterit progressive with *estar*). The data aimed to identify the diachronic changes in the factors that predict the use of these forms. The analysis was drawn from literary works from Medieval Spanish, Golden Age Spanish, and Modern Spanish to trace the development of these forms.

The results indicated that the preterit and imperfect were the most frequent forms in the data. Additionally, the factors that favor their use changed through time, which could explain why grammar analyses vary diachronically (Delgado-Díaz, 2014), as suggested by Poplack and Dion (2009). It was argued that these changes may have been caused by the emergence of the past progressive forms. This hypothesis is supported by the fact that there are many forms competing within the progressive aspectual domain. Finally, the analysis revealed that the preterit and imperfect are not opposites. The preterit conveys specific semantic functions which may not be expressed by the imperfect and vice versa.

Following Grammaticalization Theory, the following hypotheses can be stated: first, the grammaticalization order of the progressives. It was

Discussion and conclusions 127

argued that the progressive constructions emerged in the present. Then, the progressive construction extended to the imperfect and, lastly, to the preterit. Additionally, the extension of the progressive construction from present to the imperfect was due to analogy since both can express a progressive function. The extension from imperfect to preterit occurred when progressive constructions became generalized. Third, it was suggested that lexical semantics contributed to the perfect-to-perfective grammaticalization of the present perfect. Recall that the present perfect with a perfective function was used frequently with achievement and accomplishment verbs. It was hypothesized that the present perfect with accomplishment and achievement verbs was reanalyzed as perfective by an analogy with the preterit, which is used prototypically with these types of verbs. Fourth, we argue that tense, aspect, and mood[2] investigation should focus on function, rather than on form. However, further investigations are needed to fully support these hypotheses, which will allow us to have a better understanding of grammaticalization processes. Furthermore, these implications may apply to other languages as well, since the predictions of Grammaticalization Theory are cross-linguistic (Bybee et al., 1994). Additionally, these implications regarding Grammaticalization Theory can be used to explain second language acquisition processes (Galarza, forthcoming). Galarza (forthcoming) found that Spanish second language learners tend to variate before including new forms and function into their interlanguage.

In conclusion, based on the results of the present investigation, it is argued that investigating tense and aspect phenomena in dichotomous pairs (i.e., preterit vs imperfect, preterit vs present perfect, etc.) may not fully account for the range of variation since multiple forms can interact within a particular aspectual domain (Delgado-Díaz, 2018a, in press). Additionally, the results showed that the preterit and imperfect are not as stable as previously thought since they are prone to language variation and change. Moreover, it was suggested that the progressive domain appears to be the area more susceptible to variation because several forms can express this aspectual function. In addition, this research made several methodological recommendations to investigate tense and aspect, and mood (Galarza, forthcoming). For instance, it was argued that variationist analysis regarding the present perfect should use aspectual function as the dependent variable. This analysis avoids including variable and non-variable contexts in the analysis and it provides the factors that favor the use of the present perfect with a perfective function. Additionally, this methodology avoids the form-function asymmetry assumption and accounts for possible neutralized contexts (Poplack, 2018). Consequently, it is argued that tense, mood, and aspect phenomena should focus on functional domains (Delgado-Díaz, 2018a, in press; Galarza, forthcoming). Finally, the present study made several contributions to Grammaticalization Theory: first, past progressive tends to grammaticalize later than present ones, as hypothesized by Torres Cacoullos (personal communication). Second, it was hypothesized that progressive constructions spread from present to the imperfect and, lastly, to the preterit by analogy processes. Third, the emergence of these progressive constructions causes instances of layering in the progressive domain. Lastly, the emergence of past progressive constructions may have caused a shift in the Spanish aspectual system. However, there is much that remains to be uncovered with respect to Grammaticalization Theory. Bybee et al. (1994) stated that further investigations with different languages and dialects are needed to fully understand grammaticalization processes. Therefore, Grammaticalization Theory is a fertile area of research which still requires further rigorous and innovative investigations.

Notes

1 Recall that the present perfect was included only if it conveyed a perfective aspectual function.
2 See Galarza (forthcoming) for evidence which supports investigating mood focusing on function.

Bibliography

Aaron, Jessi. 2006. *Variation and Change in Spanish Future Temporal Expression: Rates, Constraints, and Grammaticization*. New Mexico, NM: The University of New Mexico dissertation.
Acero, Juan J. 1990. Las ideas de Reichenbach acerca del tiempo verbal. *Tiempo y Aspecto*, ed. by Ignacio Bosque, 45–75. Madrid: Cátedra.
Alcina Franch, Juan, and Juan Manuel Blecua. 1975. *Gramática Española*. Barcelona: Editorial Ariel.
Amaral, Patricia, and Chad Howe. 2011. Detours along the perfect path. *Selected Papers from the 39th Linguistic Symposium on Romance Languages*, ed. by Sonia Colina, Antxon Olarrea, and Ana Maria Carvalho, 387–404. Somerville, MA: Cascadilla Proceedings Project.
Amaral, Patricia, and Chad Howe. 2012. Nominal and verbal plurality in the diachrony of the Portuguese Present Perfect. *Verbal Plurality and Distributivity*, ed. by Hofherr, Patricia Cabredo, and Brenda Laca, 25–53. De Gruyter.
Andersen, Roger, and Yasuhiro Shirai. 1996. Primacy of aspect in language acquisition. *Handbook of Second Language Acquisition*, ed. by William Ritchie and Tej Bathia, 527–570. San Diego, CA: Academic Press.
Aponte-Alequín, Héctor, and Luis Ortiz-López. 2010. Una perspectiva pragmática del presente progresivo con valor de futuro en el español del Caribe. *Selected Proceedings of the 12th Hispanic Linguistics* Symposium, ed. by Claudia Borgonovo et al., 109–121. Somerville, MA: Cascadilla Proceedings Project.
Ayres, Jennifer. 2009. *El discurso de pasado del español méxico-americano en houston: un cambio lingüístico en una situación de contacto*. Houston, TX: University of Houston dissertation.
Baayen, Harald. 2008. *Analyzing Linguistic Data: A Practical Introduction to Statistics Using R*. Cambridge: Cambridge University Press.
Baker, Jennifer, and Margaret L. Quesada. 2011. The effect of temporal adverbials in the selection of preterit and imperfect by learners of Spanish L2. *Selected Proceedings of the 2009 Second Language Research Forum*, ed. by Luke Plonsky and Maren Schierloh, 1–15. Somerville, MA: Cascadilla Proceedings Project.

Bardovi-Harlig, Kathleen. 2000. *Tense and Aspect in Second Language Acquisition: Form, Meaning and Use*. Oxford: Blackwell.
Bello, Andrés. 1847 [1914]. *Gramática de la Lengua Castellana Destinada al Uso de los Americanos*. París: R. Roger and F. Chernoviz.
Bender, Andrea, Giovanni Bennardo and Sieghard Beller. 2005. Spatial frames of reference for temporal relations: A conceptual analysis in English, German, and Tongan. *Proceedings of the 27th Annual Conference of the Cognitive Science Society Mahwah*, ed. by B. G. Bara, L. Barsalou, & M. Bucciarelli, 220–225. Bucciarelli, NJ: Lawrence Erlbaum.
Bonilla, Carrie L. 2011. The conversational historical present in oral Spanish narratives. *Hispania* 94 (3). 429–442.
Brucart, Josep M. 2003. El valor del imperfecto de indicativo en español. *Estudios hispánicos. Revista de la Asociación Coreana de Hispanistas* 27. 193–233.
Burgo, Clara. 2010. A case of grammaticalization in the use of the perfect for the preterite in Bilbao Spanish. *Studies in Hispanic and Lusophone Linguistics* 3 (2). 301–328.
Bybee, Joan. 2003a. Mechanisms of change in grammaticization: The role of frequency. *The Handbook of Historical Linguistics*, ed. by Brian D. Joseph and Richard D. Janda, 602–623. Oxford: Blackwell.
Bybee, Joan. 2003b. Cognitive processes in grammaticalization. *The new psychology of language*, vol. 2, ed. by Michael Tomasello, 145–167. Mahwah, NJ: Lawrence Erlbaum.
Bybee, Joan. 2007. *Frequency of Use and the Organization of Language*. Oxford: Oxford University Press.
Bybee, Joan. 2010. *Language, Use and Cognition*. Cambridge: Cambridge University Press.
Bybee, Joan. 2015. *Language Change*. Cambridge: Cambridge University Press.
Bybee, Joan, Revere Perkins, and William Pagliuca. 1994. *The Evolution of Grammar: Tense, Aspect, and Modality in the Languages of the World*. Chicago and London: The University of Chicago Press.
Bybee, Joan, and Rena Torres Cacoullos. 2009. The role of prefabs in grammaticization: How the particular and the general interact in language change. *Formulaic Language, Volume 1, Distribution and Historical Change*, ed. by Roberta L. Corrigan, Edith A. Moravcsik, Hamid Ouali, and Kathleen Wheatley, 187–217. Amsterdam: John Benjamins.
Champion, James. 1973. Imperfect vs. preterit: A not-so-new approach. *Hispania* 56 (4). 1043–1044.
Chaston, John. 1991. Imperfect progressive usage patterns in the speech of Mexican American bilinguals from Texas. *Sociolinguistics of the Spanish-Speaking World: Iberia, Latin America, United States*. 299–311.
Cipria, Alicia and Craige Roberts. 2000. Spanish imperfecto and pretérito: Truth conditions and Aktionsart effects in a situation semantics. *Natural Language Semantics* 8. 297–347.
Claes, Jeroen, and Luis Ortiz-López. 2011. Restricciones pragmáticas y sociales en la expresión de futuridad en el español de Puerto Rico. *Spanish in Context* 8 (1). 50–72.

Bibliography 131

Comrie, Bernard. 1976. *Aspect*. Cambridge: Cambridge University Press.
Copple, Mary. 2011. Tracking the constraints on a grammaticalizing perfect (ive). *Language Variation and Change* 23 (2). 163–191.
Cortés-Torres, Mayra. 2005. ¿Qué estás haciendo? La variación de la perífrasis estar + -ndo en el español puertorriqueño. *Selected Proceedings of the 7th Hispanic Linguistics Symposium*, ed. by David Eddington, 42–55. Somerville, MA: Cascadilla Proceedings Project.
Cuza, Alejandro. 2010. The L2 acquisition of aspectual properties in Spanish. *Canadian Journal of Linguistics / Revue Canadienne de Linguistique* 55 (2). 181–208.
De Miguel, Elena. 1999. El aspecto léxico. *Gramática descriptiva de la lengua española*, ed. by Ignacio Bosque and Violeta Demonte, 2977–3060. Madrid: Espasa.
Delgado-Díaz, Gibran. 2014. Teoría vs. uso: Análisis sobre el pretérito y el imperfecto. *Boletín de Filología* 49 (1). 11–36.
Delgado-Díaz, Gibran. 2018a. *The Expression of the Past: A Variationist Analysis*. Indiana, IN: Indiana University dissertation.
Delgado-Díaz, Gibran. 2018b. Dialectal variation of the preterit and imperfect. *Revista Española de Lingüística Aplicada* 31 (1). 64–93. Amsterdam: John Benjamins.
Delgado-Díaz, Gibran. In press. Form-function asymmetry: An example from Spanish past time expressions.
Delgado-Díaz, Gibran, and Iraida Galarza. 2019. El imperfecto progresivo en el español de Puerto Rico: ¿Un caso de contacto lingüístico o gramaticalización? [The imperfect progressive in Puerto Rican Spanish: Language contact or grammaticalization?] Conference presentation, *Hispanic Linguistic Symposium*, El Paso, TX.
Delgado-Díaz, Gibran, and Luis Ortiz-López. 2011. The past tense in the Caribbean. *Cuadernos de Lingüística de la Universidad de Puerto Rico* 3 (1).
Delgado Díaz, Gibran, and Luis A. Ortiz-López. 2012. El pretérito vs. el imperfecto: ¿adquisición aspectual o temporal en 2L1 (criollo/español) y L2 (español)? *Selected Proceedings of the 14th Hispanic Linguistics Symposium*, ed. by Kimberly Geeslin and Manuel Díaz-Campos, 165–178. Somerville, MA: Cascadilla Proceedings Project.
Díaz-Campos, Manuel, Iraida Galarza, and Gibran Delgado-Díaz. 2016. The sociolinguistic profile of *ser* and *estar* in Cuban Spanish: An analysis of oral speech. *Contemporary Approaches to Cuban Spanish Dialectology*, ed. by A. Cuza, 135–159. Georgetown University Press.
Doiz, Aintzane. 2011. The Spanish preterite and imperfect from a cognitive point of view. *Research Design and Methodology in Studies on L2 Tense and Aspect*, ed. by Rafael Salaberry and Llorenç Comajoan, 55–88. Houston, TX: De Gruyter.
Domínguez, Laura, María J. Arche, and Florence Myles. 2010. Testing the predictions of the feature assembly hypothesis: Evidence from the L2 acquisition of Spanish aspect morphology. *BUCLD* 35. 183–196.

Dowty, David. 1972. Temporally restrictive adjectives. *Syntax and Semantics* 1. 51–62.
Dowty, David. 1977. Toward a semantic analysis of verb aspect and the English 'imperfective'progressive. *Linguistics and Philosophy* 1 (1). 45–77.
Dowty, David. 1979. Word meaning and Montague Grammar: The semantics of verbs and times in generative semantics and in Montague's PTQ. *Studies in Linguistics and Philosophy*. Dordrecht, Holland: D. Dordrecht: Reidel.
Dowty, David. 1986. The effects of aspectual class on the temporal structure of discourse: Semantics or pragmatics? *Linguistics and Philosophy* 9 (1). 37–61.
Dumont, Jenny. 2013. Another look at the present perfect in an Andean variety of Spanish: Grammaticalization and evidentiality in Quiteño Spanish. *Selected Proceedings of the 16th Hispanic Linguistics Symposium*, ed. by Jennifer Cabrelli Amaro et al., 279–291. Somerville, MA: Cascadilla Proceedings Project.
Erker, Daniel, and Gregory Guy. 2012. The role of lexical frequency in syntactic variability: Variable subject personal pronoun expression in Spanish. *Language* 88 (3). 526–557.
Escobar, Anna María. 1997. Contrastive and innovative uses of the present perfect and the preterite in Spanish in contact with Quechua. *Hispania* 80 (4). 859–870.
Evans, Vyvyan. 2006. *The Structure of Time: Language, Meaning and Temporal Cognition*. Amsterdam: John Benjamins.
Fafulas, Stephen. 2013. *First and Second-Language Patterns of Variation: Acquisition and Use of Simple Present and Present Progressive Forms in Spanish and English*. Indiana, IN: Indiana University dissertation.
Fafulas, Stephen. 2016. Progressive constructions in native-speaker and adult-acquired Spanish. *Studies in Hispanic and Lusophone Linguistics* 8(1). 85–133.
Fetzer, Anita, and Marjut Johansson. 2010. Cognitive verbs in context: A contrastive analysis of English and French argumentative discourse. *International Journal of Corpus Linguistics* 15 (2). 240–266.
Filip, Hana. 2011. Aspectual class and aktionsart. *Semantics: An International Handbook of Natural Language Meaning*, ed. by Claudia Maienborn, Klaus von Heusinger, and Paul Portner. De Gruyter Mouton.
Galarza, Iraida. Forthcoming. *La Adquisición de la Expresión Modal en Español de L2*. Indiana, IN: Indiana University dissertation.
García-Fernández, Luis. 2014. *El tiempo en la gramática*. Madrid: Arco Libros.
García-Negroni, María. 1999. La distinción pretérito perfecto simple / pretérito perfecto compuesto. Un enfoque discursivo. *Discurso y Sociedad* 1 (2). 45–60.
Gonzales, Patrick. 1995. Progressive and non-progressive imperfects in Spanish discourse. *Hispanic Linguistics* 6 (7). 61–92.
Gutiérrez-Araus, Mari Luz. 1998. Sistema y discurso en las formas verbales del pasado. *Revista Española de Lingüística* 28 (2). 275–306.
Harris, Martin. 1982. The 'past simple' and 'present perfect' in Romance. *Studies in the Romance verb*, ed. by Martin Harris and Nigel Vincent, 42–70. London: Croom Helm.

Heine, Bernd. 2003. Grammaticalization. *The Handbook of Historical Linguistics*, ed. by Brain Joseph and Richard Janda, 575–601. Oxford: Blackwell.
Helle, Philipp. 2006. *A Contrastive Analysis of Perception Verbs in English and German*. Northerstedt, Germany: Verlag.
Henderson, Carlos. 2010. *El pretérito perfecto compuesto del español de Chile, Paraguay y Uruguay: Aspectos semánticos y discursivos*. Stockholm, SE: Stockholm University disseratation.
Hernández, José E. 2004. *Present Perfect Variation and Grammaticalization in Salvadoran Spanish*. New Mexico, NM: The University of New Mexico dissertation.
Hernández, José E. 2008. Present Perfect semantics and usage in Salvadoran Spanish. *Revista Internacional de Lingüística Iberoamericana* 6 (2). 115–137.
Holmes, Bonnie C., and Colleen Balukas. 2011. Yesterday, all my troubles have seemed (PP) so far away: Variation in pre-hodiernal perfective expression in Peninsular Spanish. *Selected Proceedings of the 5th Workshop on Spanish Sociolinguistics*, ed. by Jim Michnowicz and Robin Dodsworth, 79–89. Somerville, MA: Cascadilla Proceedings Project.
Hopper, Paul. 1979. Aspect and foregrounding in discourse. *Syntax and Semantics* 12. 213–241. New York: Academic Press.
Hopper, Paul and Elizabeth C. Traugott. 2003. *Grammaticalization*. Cambridge: Cambridge University Press.
Howe, Chad. 2006. *Cross-Dialectal Features of the Spanish Present Perfect: A Typological Analysis of Form and Function*. Ohio, OH: Ohio State University dissertation.
Howe, Chad. 2013. *The Spanish Perfects: Pathways of Emergent Meaning [Palgrave Studies in Language Variation Series]*. Basingstoke/New York: Palgrave Macmillan.
Howe, Chad, and Scott A. Schwenter. 2008. Variable constraints on past reference in dialects of Spanish. *Selected Proceedings of the 4th Workshop on Spanish Sociolinguistics*, ed. by Maurice Westmoreland and Juan Antonio Thomas, 100–108. Somerville, MA: Cascadilla Proceedings Project.
Ibarretxe-Antuñano, Iraide. 1999. *Polysemy and Metaphor in Perception Verbs: A Cross-Linguistic Study*. Edinburgh, UK: University of Edinburgh dissertation.
Jara-Yupanqui, Margarita. 2017. The present perfect in Peruvian Spanish: An analysis of personal experience narratives among migrant generations in Lima. *Cahiers Chronos* (29). 42–78.
Jara-Yupanqui, Ileana, and Pilar Valenzuela Bismarck. 2013. El uso del perfecto en secuencias narrativas en el español peruano amazónico. *Lexis* xxxvii (i). 31–70.
Johnson, Daniel. 2009. Getting off the Goldvarb standard: Introducing Rbrul for mixed-effects variable rule analysis. *Language and Linguistics Compass*, 3 (1), 359–383.
Kanwit, Matt, Kimberly Geeslin, and Stephen Fafulas. 2015. Study abroad and the SLA of variable structures: A look at the present perfect, the copula

contrast, and the present progressive in Mexico and Spain. *Probus* 27 (2). 307–348.
King, Larry, and Margarita Suñer. 1980. The meaning of the progressive in Spanish and Portuguese. *Bilingual Review/Revista bilingüe* 7 (3). 222–238.
Koontz-Garboden, A. 1999. Covert interference in a Midwestern U.S. Spanish verbal system. Paper presented at *New Ways of Analyzing Variation (NWAV)* 28, October 17, 1999. Toronto, Ontario.
Laca, Brenda. 2006. Indefinites, quantifiers and pluractionals: What scope effects tell us about event pluralities. *Non-definiteness and plurality*, ed by Vogeleer Svetlana, and Liliane Tasmowski. Amsterdam: John Benjamins.
Lamanna, Scott. 2008. Usage of imperfect and imperfect progressive verb forms in Spanish as a majority and minority language: Is there an effect for language contact? *Selected Proceedings of the 10th Hispanic Linguistics Symposium*, ed. by Joyce Bruhn de Garavito and Elena Valenzuela, 251–264. Somerville, MA: Cascadilla Proceedings Project.
Lamanna, Scott. 2012. *Colombian Spanish in North Carolina: The Role of Language and Dialect Contact in the Formation of a New Variety of U.S. Spanish*. Indiana, IN: Indiana University dissertation.
Larson-Hall, Jenifer. 2010. *A Guide to Doing Statistics in Second Language Research Using SPSS*. New York and London: Routledge.
Levshina, Natalia. 2015. *How To Do Statistics with R: Data Exploration and Statistical Analysis*. Amsterdam: John Benjamins.
Llorach, E. Alarcos. 1947. Perfecto simple y compuesto en español. *Revista de Filología Española* 31. 108–139.
Lope Blanch, Juan M. 1972 [1961]. Sobre el uso del pretérito en el español de México. *Estudios sobre el español de México*. México: Universidad National Autónoma de México (UNAM) .
López-Otero, Julio C., and Alejandro Cuza. 2020. The distribution and use of present and past progressive forms in Spanish-English and Spanish-Brazilian Portuguese bilinguals. *Hispanic Contact Linguistics: Theoretical, methodological and empirical perspectives*, ed by Luis Ortiz-López, Rosa Guzzardo-Tamargo, and Melvin González-Rivera. Amsterdam/Philadelphia: John Benjamins.
Mayberry, María. 2011. Synchronous narratives in Spanish: The simple present/ present. *Hispania* 94 (3). 462–482.
McEnery, Tony, and Andrew Wilson. 2001. *Corpus Linguistics: An Introduction*. Edinburgh: Edinburgh University Press.
Menegotto, Andrea. 2008. Variación dialectal en los pretéritos simple y compuesto del español. *Lengua viva: Estudios ofrecidos a César Hernández Alonso* 175–201.
Michnowicz, Jim, Scott Despain, and Rebecca Gorham. In press. The changing system of Costa Rican pronouns of address: Tuteo, voseo, and usedeo. *Forms of Address in the Spanish of the Americas*, ed. by Susana Rivera-Mills and María Irene Moyna. Amsterdam: John Benjamins.

Montero Cádiz, Manuel. M. 2015. Acercamiento al empleo del pretérito perfecto compuesto del modo indicativo en la variedad cubana del español. *Revista Nebrija de Lingüística Aplicada*, 18.
Montrul, Silvina. 2002. Incomplete acquisition and attrition of Spanish tense/ aspect distinctions in adult bilinguals. *Bilingualism: Language and Cognition* 5 (1). 39–68.
Montrul, Silvina, and Roumyana Slabakova. 2000. Acquiring semantic properties of preterite and imperfect tenses in L2 Spanish. *Proceedings of the Boston University Conference on Language Development XXIV*. Cascadilla Press Proceedings.
Montrul, Silvina, and Roumyana Slabakova. 2003. Competence similarities between native and near-native speakers: An investigation of the preterit/ imperfect contrast. *Studies in Second Language Acquisition* 25. 351–398.
Mrak, Ariana. 1998. El discurso de pasado en el español de Houston: Imperfectividad y perfectividad verbal en una situación de contacto. *Southwest Journal of linguistics* 17 (2). 115–128.
Nicolle, Steve. 2012. Diachrony and grammaticalization. *The Oxford Handbook of Tense and Aspect*, ed. by Robert Binnick, 370–397. New York, NY: Oxford University Press.
Ocampo, Alicia Martini. 2008. *The Present Perfect in Spanish: A Study on Semantic Variation*. California, CA: University of South California dissertation.
Penny, Ralph. 2000. *Gramática histórica del español*. Barcelona: Ariel.
Poplack, Shana. 2011. Grammaticalization and linguistic variation. *The Oxford Handbook of Grammaticalization*, ed. by Bernd Heine and Heiko Narrog, 209–224. Oxford: Oxford University Press.
Poplack, Shana. 2018. Categories of grammar and categories of speech: When the quest for symmetry meets inherent variability. *Questioning Theoretical Primitives in Linguistic Inquiry: Papers in honor of Ricardo Otheguy*, ed. by Naomi Lapidus-Shin and Daniel Erker, 7–32. Amsterdam: John Benjamins.
Poplack, Shana, and Nathalie Dion. 2009. Prescription vs. praxis: The evolution of future temporal reference in French. *Language* 85(3). 557–587.
Poplack, Shana, and Sali Tagliamonte. 1999. Nothing in context: Variation, grammaticalization and past time marking in Nigerian Pidgin English. *Cuardenos de filología inglesa* 8. 193–217.
Pousada, Alicia, and Shana Poplack. 1979. No case for convergence: The Puerto Rican Spanish verb system in a language contact situation. *Bilingual Education for Hispanics in the United States*, ed. by Joshua Fishman and Gary Keller, 207–237. New York: Teachers College Press.
Quesada, Luis. 1993. Els drets lingüístics en l'àmbit de les ràdios municipals: Especial referència a la Comunitat Valenciana dins del nou marc comunitari europeu. *Revista de llengua i dret* 20. 61–80.
Quesada, Margaret Lubbers. 2013. The primacy of morphology in the acquisition of tense and aspect in L2 Spanish narrative structure. *Selected Proceedings of the 15th Hispanic Linguistics Symposium*, ed. by Chad Howe et al., 62–77. Somerville, MA: Cascadilla Proceedings Project.

RAE. 1973. *Esbozo de una Nueva Gramática Española.* Madrid: España.
RAE. 2010. *Nueva Gramática de la Lengua Española.* Madrid: España.
Ramos-Pellicia, Michelle. 1999. Progressive constructions in the Spanish spoken in Puerto Rico. *The Ohio State University Working Papers in Linguistics* 52. 97–112.
Reyes, Graciela. 1990. Valores estilísticos del imperfecto. *Revista de Filología Española* LXX (1/2). 45–70.
Rodríguez, Joshua. 2004. *Interpreting the Spanish Imperfecto: Issues of Aspect, Modality, Tense, and Sequence of Tense.* Ohio, OH: The Ohio State University dissertation.
Rodríguez-Louro, Celeste. 2009. *Perfect Evolution and Change: A Sociolinguistic Study of Preterit and Present Perfect Usage in Contemporary and Earlier Argentina.* Melbourne, AU: University of Melbourne dissertation.
Rodríguez-Louro, Celeste. 2010. Past time reference and the present perfect in Argentinian Spanish. *Selected Papers from the 2009 Conference of the Australian Linguistic Society*, ed. by Yvonne Treis and Rik De Busser, 1–25.
Rodríguez-Louro, Celeste, and Chad Howe. 2010. Semantic change in narrative contexts across Spanish. *Revista Internacional de Lingüística Iberoamericana* 8 (2) (16). 157–174.
Rodríguez-Louro, Celeste, and Margarita Jara-Yupanqui. 2011. Otra mirada a los procesos de gramaticalización del Presente Perfecto en español: Perú y Argentina. *Studies in Hispanic and Lusophone Linguistics* 4 (1). 55–80.
Rodríguez-Ramalle, Teresa María. 2005. *Manual de sintaxis del español.* Madrid: Castalia.
Rojas, José. 2015. *Pretérito vs. imperfecto: variación en la producción lingüística de los mexicanos en el sur de Luisiana.* Louisiana, LA: Louisiana State University dissertation.
Salaberry, Rafael. 2003. Tense aspect in verbal morphology. *Hispania*, 559–573.
Salas-González, Edelmiro. 1996. *A Semantics for the Spanish Perfective and Imperfective Forms.* California, CA: University of California, Davis dissertation.
Salas-González, Edelmiro. 1998. Spanish aspect and the nature of linguistic time. *Hispania* 81(1). 155–165.
Sankoff, David. 1988. Sociolinguistics and syntactic variation. *Linguistics: The Cambridge Survey.* 140–161.
Schwenter, Scott A. 1994. The grammaticalization of an anterior in progress: Evidence from a peninsular Spanish dialect. *Studies in Language* 18 (1). 71–111.
Schwenter, Scott A., and Rena Torres Cacoullos. 2008. Defaults and indeterminacy in temporal grammaticalization: The 'perfect' road to perfective. *Language Variation and Change* 20. 1–39.
Scrivner, Olga, and Manuel Díaz-Campos. 2016. Language variation suite: A theoretical and methodological contribution for linguistic data analysis. *Proceedings of the Linguistic Society of America* 1. 1–15.
Serrano, María José. 1996. Accounting for morpho-syntactic change in Spanish: The present perfect case. (N)WAVES and MEANS: A selection of papers from NWAVE 24. 51–61.

Serrano, María José. 2006. *Gramática del discurso*. Madrid: Akal-Cambridge.
Silva-Corvalán, Carmen. 1983. Tense and aspect in oral Spanish narrative: Context and meaning. *Language* 59 (4). 760–780.
Silva-Corvalán, Carmen. 1984. A speech event analysis of tense and aspect in Spanish. *Papers from the XIIth Linguistic Symposium on Romance Languages, University Park*, ed. by Philip Baldi, 229–251. Amsterdam/Philadelphia: John Benjamins.
Silva-Corvalán, Carmen. 1994. *Language Contact and Change*. Oxford: Oxford University Press.
Slabakova, Roumyana. 2002. Recent research on the acquisition of aspect: An embarrassment of riches? *Second Language Research* 18 (2). 172–188.
Slabakova, Roumyana, and Montrul Silvana. 1999. Aspectual tense in Spanish L2 acquisition: A UG perspective. *Tense-Aspect Morphology*, ed. by Yasuhiro Shirai and Rafael Salaberry. Benjamins Publishing Company.
Solé, Carlos and Yolanda Solé. 1976. *Modern Spanish Syntax: A Study in Contrast*. Lexington: D.C. Heath and Company.
Solé, Yolanda. 1990. Valores aspectuales en el español. *Hispanic Linguistics* 4 (1). 57–86.
Soto, Guillermo. 2011. Estructura narrativa y proyecciones entre situaciones homogéneas y discretas: Léxico, gramática y coerción. *Lenguas Modernas* 37. 109–125.
Tagliamonte, Sali. 2012. *Variationist Sociolinguistics. Change, Observation, Interpretation*. Oxford: Wiley-Blackwell.
Tagliamonte, Sali, and Harald Baayen. 2012. Models, forests and trees of York English: Was/were variation as a case study for statistical practice. *Language Variation and Change* 24 (2). 135–178.
Thomason, Sarah, and Terrence Kaufman. 1988. *Language Contact, Creolization, and Genetic Linguistics*. Berkeley, Los Angeles: University of California Press.
Torres Cacoullos, Rena. 2000. *Grammaticization, Synchronic Variation, and Language Contact. A Study of Spanish Progressive -ndo Constructions*. Amsterdam/Philadelphia: John Benjamins.
Torres Cacoullos, Rena. 2009. Variation and grammaticisation: The emergence of an aspectual opposition. *Studies in Language Variation: European Perspectives II*, ed. by Stavroula Tsiplakou, Marilena Karyolemou, and Pavlos Pavlou, 215–224. Amsterdam: John Benjamins.
Torres Cacoullos, Rena. 2011. Variation and grammaticalization. *The Handbook of* Hispanic Sociolinguistics, ed. by Manuel Díaz Campos. Malden, MA: Wiley-Blackwell.
Torres Cacoullos, Rena. 2012. Grammaticalization through inherent variability: The development of a progressive in Spanish. *Studies in Language* 36 (1). 73–122.
Torres Cacoullos, Rena. 2015. Gradual loss of analyzability: Diachronic priming effects. *Variation in Language: System- and Usage-Based Approaches*, ed. by Aria Adli, Göz Kaufmann, and Marco García, 267–289. Berlin: De Gruyter.
Van Ess-Dykema, Carol. 1984. *The Historical Present in Oral Spanish Narratives*. Washington, DC: Georgetown University Press.

Vendler, Zeno. 1957. Verb and times. *The Philosophical Review* 66 (2). 143–160.
Verkuyl, Henke J. 1972. *On the Compositional Nature of the Aspects (Vol. 15)*. Dordrecht: D. Reidel Publishing Company.
Verkuyl, Henke J. 2005. Aspectual composition: Surveying the ingredients. *Perspectives on Aspect. Studies in Theoretical Psycholinguistics 32*, ed. by Henk Verkuyl, Henriette de Swart, and Angeliek van Hout, 19–39. Dordrecht: Springer.
Verkuyl, Henke J. 2012 Compositionality. *The Oxford Handbook of Tense and Aspect*, ed. by Robert Binnick, 563–585. Oxford: Oxford University Press.
Weinrich, Harald. 1968. *Estructura y función de los tiempos en el lenguaje*. Madrid: Gredos.
Westfall, Ruth. 1995. *Simple and Progressive Forms of the Spanish Past Tense System: A Semantic and Pragmatic Study in Viewpoint Contrast*. Texas, TX: University of Texas at Austin dissertation.
Westfall, Ruth. 2003. Simple and progressive forms of the perfective viewpoint in Spanish: The preterit and the preterit progressive. *Hispania* 86 (40). 874–888.
Zentella, Ana Celia. 1997. *Growing Up Bilingual: Puerto Rican Children in New York*. Oxford: Blackwell.

Index

animacy of the subject 71
aspect 1–5; habitual 1, 3, 9, 54–5, 62–3, 114, 116–18; non-progressive 3–4; perfective 1–3, 18, 24, 25, 34, 40, 55, 62–3, 114, 116–18, 120–2; progressive 2–4, 55, 62–3, 113–19, 124–5

conditional trees 78

discourse hypothesis 7, 31, 33, 37; background information 7–8, 31, 37–9, 44, 49–51, 56, 65–6, 80, 84, 87; foreground information 7–8, 31–3, 37–8, 44–6, 53–4, 56, 65–6, 87, 95–7

form-function asymmetry 4–5, 25, 53, 118–19
form-function symmetry doctrine 63
frame of temporal reference 66; absolute 66–8; indeterminate 20, 66–8; intrinsic 66–8; irrelevant 20, 66–7; relative 66–8

Golden Age Spanish 59–60
grammatical person 72
grammaticalization 11–23, 116, 119–20, 122, 124–5; analogy 14, 121, 124, 127–2; decategorization 12–13; erosion 12–13; generalization 12, 14, 51, 57, 124; layering 13, 17, 20, 55, 116, 118, 128; reanalysis 14; retention 13–14, 20, 55; semantic bleaching 12–13, 18
grammaticalization path 16, 120

Grammaticalization Theory 2, 11, 15–16, 18, 21, 23, 43, 46, 51, 58, 73, 75, 122, 126–8

lexical aspect 5–6; accomplishment verbs 6, 64, 120–2, 127; achievement verbs 6–7, 64–5, 120–1; activity verbs 6, 8, 30, 64; cognitive verbs 7, 64–5; perception verbs 7, 64–5; state verbs 7, 64; *see also* lexical semantics 5, 8, 64, 127
lexical aspect hypothesis 6
lexical frequency 72

Medieval Spanish 59–60
Modern Spanish 59–60
multiple response set 77–8

past expressions: imperfect 1, 3–4, 6–9, 20, 33–9, 55–6, 60, 79–89, 112–14, 116–20, 126–7; imperfect progressive with *estar* 1, 6, 19, 102–6, 113, 115–17, 122–4
perfect-to-perfective grammaticalization 19, 40, 42, 44, 46, 115, 120, 122, 127; present perfect 1–2, 4, 6, 13, 17, 19–20, 39–47, 55–7, 60, 99–101, 115–18, 120–2, 127; preterit 1–2, 4, 6–10, 13, 17, 20, 24–33, 40, 42, 54–6, 60–1, 89–99, 112–14, 116–21, 126–8; preterit progressive with *estar* 4–6, 51–4, 102–6, 113, 116–17, 122–4, 126; progressive constructions with other auxiliary

140 *Index*

verbs 10, 60, 102, 106–10, 113, 115–17, 125
plurality of the direct object 70, 81, 90
priming 73–4, 79–81, 84, 86, 88–91, 95–7, 120
progressive constructions unit-hood 22; adjacency 20–1, 75, 104, 122–4; association 21, 75, 104, 122–3; co-occurrence with locative expressions 12, 20–1, 74, 104–5, 122, 124; fusion 21–2, 76, 104, 106, 122–3

specificity of the subject 9–10, 69, 91, 95, 97–8, 120

For Product Safety Concerns and Information please contact our EU representative GPSR@taylorandfrancis.com
Taylor & Francis Verlag GmbH, Kaufingerstraße 24, 80331 München, Germany